Android Sensor Programming By Example

Take your Android applications to the next level of interactivity by exploring the wide variety of Android sensors

Varun Nagpal

BIRMINGHAM - MUMBAI

Android Sensor Programming By Example

First published: April 2016

Production reference: 1270416

Published by Packt Publishing Ltd.
Livery Place
35 Livery Street
Birmingham
B3 2PB, UK.
ISBN 978-1-78528-550-9

Credits

Author

Varun Nagpal

Reviewers

Ahmed Mubarak Al-Haiqi

José Juan Sánchez Hernández

Commissioning Editor

Ashwin Nair

Acquisition Editor

Tushar Gupta

Content Development Editor

Pooja Mhapsekar

Technical Editor

Vivek Arora

Copy Editor

Angad Singh

Project Coordinator

Judie Jose

Proofreader

Safis Editing

Indexer

Mariammal Chettiyar

Graphics

Abhinash Sahu

Production Coordinator

Arvindkumar Gupta

About the Author

Varun Nagpal has been developing mobile apps since 2005 and has developed and contributed to more than 100 professional apps and games on various platforms, such as Android, iOS, Blackberry, and J2ME. Android app development has been his main area of expertise, and he has developed apps for a wide variety of Android devices, such as Android phones, tablets, watches, smart TVs, Android Auto, and Google Glass.

He moved to Chicago in late 2013, and since then, he has become a seasoned mobile architect. He has worked in different roles (mobile architect, technical lead, senior developer, and technical consultant) for a variety of various global clients (Allstate, Verizon, AT&T, Sydbank Denmark, SiS Taiwan, Chams PLC Nigeria, and Nandos South Africa) in order to implement their mobile solutions. He has SCJP (Core Java) and SCWD (JSP and Servlets) certifications from Sun Microsystems and MCP (C#) and MCTS (ASP.NET) certifications from Microsoft. You can find his blogs on mobile technology and white papers written by him on his website at `http://www.varunnagpal.com/`.

When he's not working, Varun can be found meditating or playing the flute. He also loves to develop meditation apps and fun games in his free time. He has developed about 40 meditation apps and games available on Google Play (`https://play.google.com/store/apps/developer?id=Creative.Software.Studio`) and the Apple App Store (`https://itunes.apple.com/us/artist/creative-software-studio/id574745824`) under the name of Creative Software Studio, his part-time start-up company (`http://creativesoftwarestudio.com/`).

I would like to thank my wife, Ankita, for supporting me at every step, and I want to apologize to my one-year-old daughter for not giving her enough time while writing this book. I would also like to acknowledge my parents for their encouragement. Finally, I want to thank the editor, each member of the Packt Publishing team, and the technical reviewers for the effort and enthusiasm they showed while working on this book.

About the Reviewers

Ahmed Mubarak Al-Haiqi received his PhD (he investigated sensor-based side channels on Android) and MEng (in computer and communications engineering) degrees from the National University of Malaysia. Before pursuing his graduate studies, he worked as a database developer for several years with governmental organizations in Aden, Yemen, where he completed a BEng and majored in computer engineering and science. He is currently involved in conducting academic research on mobile security, machine learning, next generation networking trends, as well as interdisciplinary topics.

José Juan Sánchez Hernández received an MSc degree in computer science from the University of Almería in 2008. He is a member of the Supercomputing-Algorithms Research Group at the University of Almería, and he is currently working toward a PhD in the area of image coding and transmission.

In his spare time, he enjoys designing and developing native mobile apps for Android, experimenting and making stuff with Arduino and Raspberry Pi, and learning new things. He is also the cofounder of Android Almería Developers Group and an active member of HackLab Almería, where he organizes programming talks and hackathons.

He participated as a mentor in the Google Summer of Code 2015 with the P2PSP organization. You can find out more about him at `http://josejuansanchez.org`.

www.PacktPub.com

For support files and downloads related to your book, please visit www.PacktPub.com.

Did you know that Packt offers eBook versions of every book published, with PDF and ePub files available? You can upgrade to the eBook version at www.PacktPub.com and as a print book customer, you are entitled to a discount on the eBook copy. Get in touch with us at service@packtpub.com for more details.

At www.PacktPub.com, you can also read a collection of free technical articles, sign up for a range of free newsletters and receive exclusive discounts and offers on Packt books and eBooks.

https://www2.packtpub.com/books/subscription/packtlib

Do you need instant solutions to your IT questions? PacktLib is Packt's online digital book library. Here, you can search, access, and read Packt's entire library of books.

Why subscribe?

- Fully searchable across every book published by Packt
- Copy and paste, print, and bookmark content
- On demand and accessible via a web browser

Free access for Packt account holders

If you have an account with Packt at www.PacktPub.com, you can use this to access PacktLib today and view 9 entirely free books. Simply use your login credentials for immediate access.

Table of Contents

Preface

Welcome to *Android Sensor Programming By Example*. This book will provide you the skills required to use sensors in your Android applications. It will walk you through all the fundamentals of sensors and will provide a thorough understanding of the Android Sensor Framework. This book will cover a wide variety of sensors available on the Android Platform. You will learn how to write code for the infrastructure (service, threads, database) required to process high volumes of sensor data. This book will also teach you how to connect and use sensors in external devices (such as Android Wear) from the Android app using the Google Fit platform.

You will learn from many real-world sensor-based applications such, as the Pedometer app to detect daily steps, the Weather app to detect temperature, altitude, absolute and humidity, the Driving app to detect risky driving behavior, and the Fitness tracker app to track heart rate, weight, daily steps, and calories burned.

What this book covers

Chapter 1, *Sensor Fundamentals*, provides you a thorough understanding of the fundamentals and framework of Android sensors. It walks you through the different types of sensors and the sensor coordinate system in detail.

Chapter 2, *Playing with Sensors*, guides you through various classes, callbacks, and APIs of the Android Sensor framework. It walks you through a sample application, which provides a list of available sensors and their values and individual capabilities, such as the range of values, power consumption, minimum time interval, and so on.

Chapter 3, *The Environmental Sensors – The Weather Utility App*, explains the usage of various environment sensors. We develop a weather utility app to compute altitude, absolute humidity, and dew point using temperature, pressure, and relative humidity sensors.

Chapter 4, *The Light and Proximity Sensors*, teaches you how to use proximity and light sensors. It explains the difference between wakeup and non-wakeup sensors and explains the concept of the hardware FIFO sensor queue. As a learning exercise, we develop a small application that turns on/off a flashlight using a proximity sensor, and it also adjusts screen brightness using a light sensor.

Chapter 5, *The Motion, Position, and Fingerprint Sensors*, explains the working principle of motion sensors (accelerometer, gyroscope, linear acceleration, gravity, and significant motion), position sensors (magnetometer and orientation), and the fingerprint sensor. We learn the implementation of these sensors with the help of three examples. The first example explains how to use the accelerometer sensor to detect phone shake. The second example teaches how to use the orientation, magnetometer, and accelerometer sensors to build a compass, and in the third example, we learn how to use the fingerprint sensor to authenticate a user.

Chapter 6, *The Step Counter and Detector Sensors – The Pedometer App*, explains how to use the step detector and step counter sensors. Through a real-world pedometer application, we learn how to analyze and process the accelerometer and step detector sensor data to develop an algorithm for detecting the type of step (walking, jogging, sprinting). We also look at how to drive the pedometer data matrix (total steps, distance, duration, average speed, average step frequency, calories burned, and type of step) from the sensor data.

Chapter 7, *The Google Fit Platform and APIs – The Fitness Tracker App*, introduces you to the new Google Fit platform. It walks you through the different APIs provided by the Google Fit platform and explains how to request automated collection and storage of sensor data in a battery-efficient manner without the app being alive in the background all the time. As a learning exercise, we develop a fitness tracker application that collects and processes the fitness sensor data, including the sensor data obtained from remotely connected Android Wear devices.

Bonus Chapter, Sensor Fusion and Sensor – Based APIs (the Driving Events Detection App), guides you through the working principle of sensor-based Android APIs (activity recognition, geo-fence, and fused location) and teaches you various aspects of sensor fusion. Through a real-world application, you will learn how to use multiple sensors along with input from sensor-based APIs to detect risky driving behavior. Through the same application, you will also learn how to develop the infrastructure (service, threads, and database) required to process high volumes of sensor data in the background for a longer duration of time. This chapter is available online at the link `https://www.packtpub.com/sites/default/files/downloads/SensorFusionandSensorBasedAPIs_TheDrivingEventDetectionApp_OnlineChapter.pdf`

What you need for this book

You will need a Windows or a Mac system with Android Studio to run the examples in this book. All the examples are developed using Android Studio, but you can still execute them on Eclipse with ADT by exporting them to an Eclipse project structure. You are encouraged to run all the examples in the book on a real Android device as there is no official support for sensors in the Android emulator. An open source sensor simulator is available, and it will simulate some of the sensors on the Android emulator in real time. It is available at `htt ps://code.google.com/p/openintents/wiki/SensorSimulator`.

Who this book is for

This book is targeted at Android developers who want to thoroughly understand sensors and write sensor-based applications or want to enhance their existing applications with additional sensor functionality. A basic knowledge of Android development is required.

Conventions

In this book, you will find a number of text styles that distinguish between different kinds of information. Here are some examples of these styles and an explanation of their meaning.

Code words in text, database table names, folder names, filenames, file extensions, pathnames, dummy URLs, user input, and Twitter handles are shown as follows: "Fingerprint sensor APIs require install time permission in the `AndroidManifest.xml` file."

A block of code is set as follows:

```
@Override
    protected void onCreate(Bundle savedInstanceState) {
        super.onCreate(savedInstanceState);
        mSensorManager = (SensorManager)
        getSystemService(Context.SENSOR_SERVICE);
        mSensor = mSensorManager.getDefaultSensor
        (Sensor.TYPE_SIGNIFICANT_MOTION);
```

New terms and **important words** are shown in bold.

 Warnings or important notes appear in a box like this.

 Tips and tricks appear like this.

Reader feedback

Feedback from our readers is always welcome. Let us know what you think about this book-what you liked or disliked. Reader feedback is important for us as it helps us develop titles that you will really get the most out of.

To send us general feedback, simply e-mail feedback@packtpub.com, and mention the book's title in the subject of your message.

If there is a topic that you have expertise in and you are interested in either writing or contributing to a book, see our author guide at www.packtpub.com/authors .

Customer support

Now that you are the proud owner of a Packt book, we have a number of things to help you to get the most from your purchase.

Downloading the example code

You can download the example code files for this book from your account at `http://www.packtpub.com`. If you purchased this book elsewhere, you can visit `http://www.packtpub.com/support` and register to have the files e-mailed directly to you.

You can download the code files by following these steps:

1. Log in or register to our website using your e-mail address and password.
2. Hover the mouse pointer on the **SUPPORT** tab at the top.
3. Click on **Code Downloads & Errata**.
4. Enter the name of the book in the **Search** box.
5. Select the book for which you're looking to download the code files.
6. Choose from the drop-down menu where you purchased this book from.
7. Click on **Code Download**.

You can also download the code files by clicking on the **Code Files** button on the book's webpage at the Packt Publishing website. This page can be accessed by entering the book's name in the **Search** box. Please note that you need to be logged in to your Packt account.

Once the file is downloaded, please make sure that you unzip or extract the folder using the latest version of:

- WinRAR / 7-Zip for Windows
- Zipeg / iZip / UnRarX for Mac
- 7-Zip / PeaZip for Linux

Errata

Although we have taken every care to ensure the accuracy of our content, mistakes do happen. If you find a mistake in one of our books-maybe a mistake in the text or the code-we would be grateful if you could report this to us. By doing so, you can save other readers from frustration and help us improve subsequent versions of this book. If you find any errata, please report them by visiting http://www.packtpub.com/submit-errata, selecting your book, clicking on the **Errata Submission Form** link, and entering the details of your errata. Once your errata are verified, your submission will be accepted and the errata will be uploaded to our website or added to any list of existing errata under the Errata section of that title.

To view the previously submitted errata, go to https://www.packtpub.com/books/content/support and enter the name of the book in the search field. The required information will appear under the **Errata** section.

Piracy

Piracy of copyrighted material on the Internet is an ongoing problem across all media. At Packt, we take the protection of our copyright and licenses very seriously. If you come across any illegal copies of our works in any form on the Internet, please provide us with the location address or website name immediately so that we can pursue a remedy.

Please contact us at `copyright@packtpub.com` with a link to the suspected pirated material.

We appreciate your help in protecting our authors and our ability to bring you valuable content.

Questions

If you have a problem with any aspect of this book, you can contact us at `questions@packtpub.com`, and we will do our best to address the problem.

1

Sensor Fundamentals

In this chapter, we will understand the fundamentals of sensors and explore what the sensor world looks like from an Android perspective. We will also look at the classes, interfaces, and methods provided by the Android platform to access sensors. This chapter will also focus on the standards and best practices for using Android sensors.

You will learn the following topics in this chapter:

- What are sensors?
- Different types of sensors and values.
- Individual sensor descriptions and their common usage.
- How to use sensor coordinate system?
- What is Android Sensor Stack?
- Understanding the Sensor framework APIs and classes.
- Understanding the sensor sampling period, frequency, and reporting mode.
- Specific sensor configuration and sensor availability based on the API level.
- Best practices to access and use sensors.

What are sensors?

In simple words, sensors measure a particular kind of physical quantity, such as force acting on device, light falling on a surface, or the temperature in a room. These are examples of a basic physical quantity that sensors can measure. Most Android phones come with advance sensors that can measure valuable information such as relative humidity, atmospheric pressure, magnetic field, steps taken, the rate of rotation of a device on the x, y, and z axes, proximity to an object, and many more. The majority of the sensors are **Micro Electro Mechanical Sensors** (**MEMS**), which are made on a tiny scale (in micrometers), usually on a silicon chip, with mechanical and electrical elements integrated together.

The basic working principle behind MEMS is to measure the change in electric signal originating due to mechanical motion. This change in electric signals is converted to digital values by electric circuits. The accelerometer and gyroscope are the main examples of MEMS. Most of the sensors in an Android phone consume minimal battery and processing power. We will discuss all the important sensors in detail in the coming chapters.

Types of sensors

Sensor can be broadly divided into the following two categories:

- **Physical Sensors**: These are the actual pieces of hardware that are physically present on the device. They are also known as hardware sensors. Accelerometers, gyroscopes, and magnetometers are examples of physical sensors.
- **Synthetic Sensors**: These are not physically present on the device, and they are instead derived from one or more sensors. They are also called virtual, composite, or software sensors. Gravity, linear acceleration, and step detector are examples of synthetic sensors.

The Android platform doesn't make any distinction when dealing with physical sensors and synthetic sensors. The distinction is mostly theoretical to understand the origin of the sensor values.

Types of sensor values

Sensor values can be broadly divided into the following three categories:

- **Raw**: These values are directly given by the sensor. The operating system simply passes these values to the apps without adding any correction logic. Accelerometers, proximity sensors, light sensors, and barometers are sensors that give raw values.

- **Calibrated**: These values are computed by the operating system by adding extra correction algorithms, such as drift compensation and removing bias and noise over the raw values given by sensors. Step detector, step counter, and significant motion are sensors that give calibrated values by using an accelerometer as their base sensor. The magnetometer and gyroscope are special kinds of sensor that give both raw and calibrated values.

- **Fused**: These values are derived from a combination of two or more sensors. Generally, these values are calculated by leveraging the strength of one sensor to accommodate the weaknesses of other sensors. Gravity and linear acceleration give fused values by using the accelerometer and gyroscope.

Motion, position, and environmental sensors

The Android platform supports mainly three broad categories of sensors: the motion, position, and environment-based sensors. This categorization is done based on the type of physical quantity detected and measured by the sensors.

Motion sensors

Motion sensors are responsible for measuring any kind of force that could potentially create motion in the x, y, and z axes of the phone. The motion could be either a linear or angular movement in any direction. This category includes accelerometers, gravity, gyroscope, and rotational vector sensors. Most of these sensors will have values in the x, y, and z axes, and the rotational vector will especially have extra value in the fourth axis, which is the scalar component of the rotation vector.

The following table summarizes the motion sensor usage, types, and power consumption:

Sensor	Type	Value	Underlying Sensors	Description	Common Usage	Power Consumption
Accelerometer	Physical	Raw	Accelerometer	This measures the acceleration force along the x, y, and z axes (including gravity). Unit: m/s^2	It can be used to detect motion such as shakes, swings, tilt, and physical forces applied on the phone.	Low
Gravity	Synthetic	Fused	Accelerometer, Gyroscope	This measures the force of gravity along the x, y, and z axes. Unit: m/s^2	It can be used to detect when the phone is in free fall.	Medium
Linear Acceleration	Synthetic	Fused	Accelerometer, Gyroscope	It measures the acceleration force along the x, y, and z axes (excluding gravity). Unit: m/s^2	It can be used to detect motion such as shakes, swings, tilt, and physical forces applied on phone.	Medium

Gyroscope	Physical	Raw, Calibrated	Gyroscope	This measures the rate of rotation of the device along the x, y, and z axes. Unit: rad/s	It can be used to detect rotation motions such as spin, turn, and any angular movement of the phone.	Medium
Step Detector	Synthetic	Calibrated	Accelerometer	This detects walking steps.	It can be used to detect when a user starts walking.	Low
Step Counter	Synthetic	Calibrated	Accelerometer	It measures the number of steps taken by the user since the last reboot while the sensor was activated	It keeps track of the steps taken by the user per day.	Low
Significant Motion	Synthetic	Calibrated	Accelerometer	It detects when there is significant motion on the phone because of walking, running, or driving.	It detects a significant motion event.	Low

Rotation Vector	Synthetic	Fused	Accelerometer, Gyroscope, Magnetometer	This measures the rotation vector component along the x axis ($x * sin(\theta/2)$), y axis ($y * sin(\theta/2)$), and z axis ($z * sin(\theta/2)$). Scalar component of the rotation vector ($(cos(\theta/2))$). Unitless.	It can be used in 3D games based on phone direction.	High

Position sensors

Position sensors are used to measure the physical position of the phone in the world's frame of reference. For example, you can use the geomagnetic field sensor in combination with the accelerometer to determine a device's position relative to the magnetic North Pole. You can use the orientation sensor to determine the device's position in your application's frame of reference. Position sensors also support values in the x,y, and z axes.

The following table summarizes the position sensor's usage, types, and power consumption:

Sensor	Type	Value	Underlying Sensors	Description	Common Usage	Power Consumption
Magnetometer	Physical	Raw, Calibrated	Magnetometer	This measures the geomagnetic field strength along the x, y, and z axes. Unit: μT	It can be used to create a compass and calculate true north.	Medium
Orientation (Deprecated)	Synthetic	Fused	Accelerometer, Gyroscope, Magnetometer	This measures the Azimuth (the angle around the z axis), Pitch (the angle around the x axis), and Roll (the angle around the y axis). Unit: Degrees	It can be used to detect the device's position and orientation.	Medium
Proximity	Physical	Raw	Proximity	This measures the distance of an object relative to the view screen of a device. Unit: cm	It can be used to determine whether a handset is being held up to a person's ear.	Low

Game Rotation Vector	Synthetic	Fused	Accelerometer, Gyroscope	This measures the rotation vector component along the x axis ($x * sin(\theta/2)$), y axis ($y * sin(\theta/2)$), and z axis ($z * sin(\theta/2)$). It is the scalar component of the rotation vector ($cos(\theta/2)$). Unitless. It is based only on the Gyroscope and Accelerometer and does not use the Magnetometer.	It can be used in 3D games based on phone direction.	Medium

| Geomagnetic Rotation Vector | Synthetic | Fused | Accelerometer, Magnetometer | This measures the rotation vector component along the x axis ($x * sin(\theta/2)$), y axis ($y * sin(\theta/2)$), and z axis ($z * sin(\theta/2)$). It is the scalar component of the rotation vector ($cos(\theta/2)$). Unit less. * It is based only on the Magnetometer and Accelerometer and does not use the Gyroscope. | It can be used in augmented reality apps, which are based on the phone and compass direction. | Medium |

Environmental sensors

Environment sensors are responsible for measuring environmental properties, such as temperature, relative humidity, light, and air pressure near the phone. Unlike motion and position sensors, which give sensor values multi-dimensional arrays, the environment sensors report single sensor values.

The following table summarizes the environment sensor's usage, types, and power consumption:

Sensor	Type	Value	Underlying Sensors	Description	Common Usage	Power Consumption
Ambient Temperature	Physical	Raw	Thermometer	This measures the ambient air temperature. Unit: Degrees Celsius	It is used for monitoring temperatures.	Medium
Light	Physical	Raw	Photometer	This measures the ambient light level (illumination). Unit: lx	It can be used to dim the screen brightness of the phone.	Low
Barometer	Physical	Raw	Barometer	This measures the ambient air pressure. Unit: mPa or mbar	It can be used to measure height relative to sea level.	Medium
Relative Humidity	Physical	Raw	Relative Humidity	This measures the relative ambient humidity in percentage. Unit: %	It can be used for calculating the dew point, and absolute and relative humidity.	Medium

Sensors' coordinate system

Most of the sensors use the standard 3-axis coordinate system to represent the sensor values. This coordinate system is similar to the 3-axis coordinate system used to measure the length, breadth, and height of any 3D object in space, along with the difference of the frame of reference and the orientation of the 3-axis. As depicted in the following figure, the origin of this coordinate system lies in the center of the screen. When the device is in its default orientation (generally the portrait mode), the x axis is in the horizontal direction with the right-hand side having positive values and the left-hand side having negative values. Similarly, the y axis is in the vertical direction and the z axis is coming out of the phone screen. Points above the origin in a vertical direction are positive, and the ones below the origin in vertical direction are negative for the y axis. Similarly, the points coming out of the screen are positive, and the points behind the phone screen are negative for the z axis.

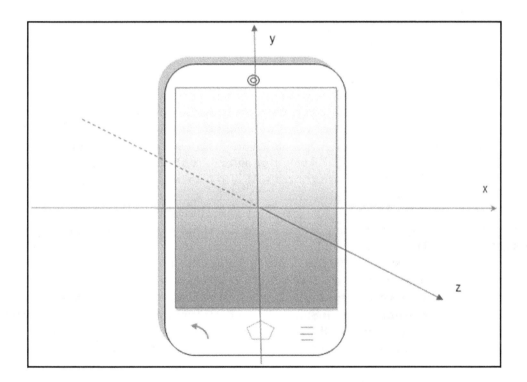

This particular x, y, and z axis orientation stands good for all the devices that have their default orientation as portrait mode, as shown in the previous figure. But for any device, especially tablets, the orientation of the x and y axes are swapped when their default orientation is in landscape mode. The z axis' orientation remains the same. So, before making any assumption about the orientation of an axis, it's always a good practice to confirm the default mode of the device. In this coordinate system, we always use the device's frame as a point of reference. The device coordinate system is never changed or swapped, especially when the phone is moved or rotated in any direction. The OpenGL (Graphic library) uses the same coordinate system and rules to define its values.

Some position sensors and their methods use a coordinate system that is relative to the world's frame of reference, as opposed to the device's frame of reference. These sensors and methods return data that represents the device motion or device position relative to the earth. The Orientation Sensor, Rotation Vector Sensor, and `getOrientation()` method use the world's frame of reference coordinate system, while all the other position, motion, and environmental sensors use the device's frame of reference coordinate system.

Android Sensor Stack

The following figure represents the layers in the Android Sensor Stack. Each layer in the sensor stack is responsible for a specific task and communicating with the next layer. The top-most layer consists of Android Apps, which are the consumers of the data from sensors. The second layer is the Android SDK layer, through which the android applications can access the sensors. The Android SDK contains APIs to list the available sensors to register to a sensor and all the other sensor functionality. The third layer consists of the Android Framework, which is in charge of linking several applications to a single HAL client. The framework consists of various components to provide simultaneous access to multiple applications. It is discussed in detail in the next section. The fourth layer is called **HAL** (Sensors' **Hardware Abstraction Layer**), which provides the interface between the hardware drivers and the Android framework. It consists of one HAL interface sensor and one HAL implementation, which we refer to as `sensors.cpp`. The HAL interface is defined by the Android and **AOSP** (**Android Open Source Project**) contributors, and the implementation is provided by the manufacturer of the device. The Sensor Drivers are the fifth layer of the stack, and they are responsible for interacting with the physical devices.

In some cases, the HAL implementation and the drivers are the same software entity, while in other cases, the hardware integrator requests the sensor chip manufacturers to provide the drivers. The Sensor Hub is the sixth optional layer of the stack. The Sensor Hub generally consists of a separate, dedicated chip for performing low-level computation at low power, while the application processor is in the suspended mode. It is generally used for sensor batching and adding hardware FIFO queue (which is discussed in detail in the *Wake locks, wakeup sensors, and FIFO queue* section of `Chapter 4`, *Light and Proximity Sensors*). The final seventh layer consists of the physical hardware sensors. Mostly, they are made up of the MEMS silicon chip, and they do the real measuring work.

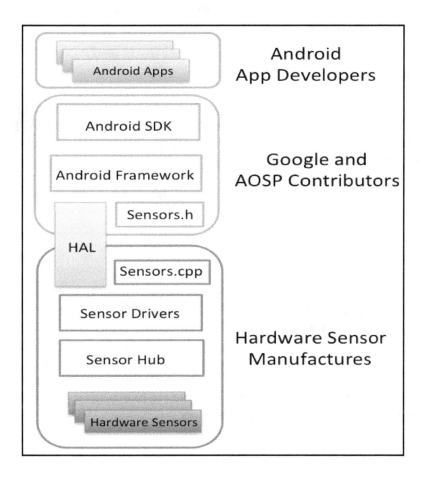

Components of the sensor framework

Android has provided methods, classes, and interfaces for accessing sensors and their data that is available on an Android device. These sets of methods, classes, and interfaces are collectively referred to as the sensor framework and are a part of the `android.hardware` package. It consists of four major components: `SensorManager`, `Sensor`, `SensorEvent`, and `SensorEventListener`. The entry point to the framework is the `SensorManager` class, which allows an app to request sensor information and register to receive sensor data. When registered, sensor data values are sent to a `SensorEventListener` interface in the form of a `SensorEvent` class that contains information produced from a given sensor. Let's look at each component in detail.

SensorManager

`SensorManager` is the class that makes it possible for your app to get access to the sensors. It creates the instance of the system sensor service, which provides various APIs to access sensor information on the device. It exposes the methods that list the available and default sensors on the device. This class also provides several sensor constants that are used to report sensor accuracy, sampling period, and calibrate sensors. One of the important tasks of this class is to register and unregister sensor event listeners for accessing a particular sensor.

SensorEventListener

`SensorEventListener` is the interface that provides two callbacks to receive the sensor notification (sensor event). `OnSensorChanged()` is the first method of the interface, which is called whenever there is any change in the sensor values. The change in sensor value is communicated through the `SensorEvent` object, passed as a parameter to this method. `OnAccuracyChanged()` is the second method, which is called whenever there is a change in the accuracy of sensor values. The sensor object and newly reported accuracy in integers are sent as parameters to this method. There are four accuracy integer constants supported by `SensorManager`. They are as follows:

- `SENSOR_STATUS_ACCURACY_HIGH`
- `SENSOR_STATUS_ACCURACY_MEDIUM`
- `SENSOR_STATUS_ACCURACY_LOW`
- `SENSOR_STATUS_ACCURACY_UNRELIABLE`

Sensor

Sensor is the class that is used to create an instance of a specific sensor. This class provides various methods that let you determine a sensor's capabilities:

- Maximum Range
- Minimum Delay
- Name
- Power
- Resolution
- Reporting Mode
- Type
- Vendor
- Version
- isWakeUp Sensor

We will be discussing each capability and method in detail in the *Time for action – knowing the individual sensor capability* section of Chapter 2, *Playing with Sensors*.

SensorEvent

SensorEvent is a special kind of class that is used by the operating system to report changes in the sensor values to the listeners. This SensorEvent object contains the following four elements:

- values[]: This is a multidimensional array that holds the sensor values
- timestamp: This refers to the time in nanoseconds at which the event happened
- accuracy: This is one of the four accuracy integer constants
- sensor: This is the sensor type that generated this data

The following class diagram depicts the important methods and variables for the four key components of the Sensor Framework:

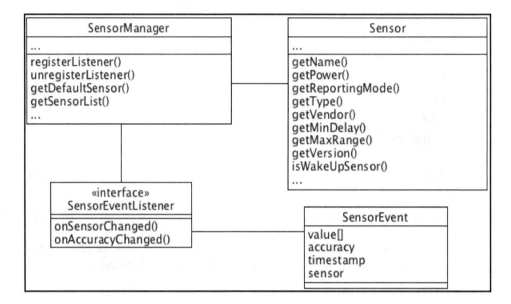

Sensor's sampling period, power, and battery consumption

When you are registering an event listener, you can suggest a sampling period or delay between the sensor event values in microseconds. This sampling period is only a signal to the operating system to send the sensor values at the suggested sampling rate via the OnSensorChanged() method. The operating system might choose a bigger delay, depending on the load on the processer, and that's why it is discouraged to build a time-sensitive logic that relies on the delay between the sensor events.

You can only specify the absolute delay from Android 3.0 (API Level 11) and above. Prior to this version, you could only use the following four constants supported by the platform:

- SENSOR_DELAY_FASTEST: This has a default value of 0 microseconds. It is not recommended to use this delay, as it increases the CPU cycles by multiple times and drains the battery much faster.
- SENSOR_DELAY_GAME: This has a default value of 20,000 microseconds. It is only recommended for those games that need the highest degree of precision and accuracy.
- SENSOR_DELAY_UI: This has a default value of 60,000 microseconds and is recommended for most cases.
- SENSOR_DELAY_NORMAL: It has a default value of 200,000 microseconds and is used for reducing the extra CPU cycles and saving the battery.

It's the choice of the developer to either use the delay constants or specify their own delay value. Power consumption and the degree of precision are the two important factors to consider before deciding the right sampling period. The power consumption of any sensor can be checked via the getPower() method of the sensor object, which returns the power in mA. Among the physical sensors, the accelerometer is the most power efficient and has the least battery consumption. The gyroscope and magnetometer come after the accelerometer with regard to power efficiency and battery consumption.

You will often hear the terms delay and sampling period being used interchangeably because they mean the same thing. There is another term called sampling frequency, which is the inverse of the sampling period (in seconds) and is measured in **Hertz (Hz)**. For example, if you are using the sampling period of 60,000 microseconds for a sensor, then the sampling frequency will be 16.66 Hz. This conversion is just a two-step process. First, convert the time into seconds, as 1 second is 10 to power 6 microseconds, so 60,000 microseconds will be 0.06 seconds. Now, the frequency (the inverse of delay) is *1/0.06 = 16.66 Hz*.

The reporting modes of sensors

Sensors can generate events in different ways called reporting modes. Each sensor has a particular type of reporting mode. The reporting mode is an Integer constant of the `Sensor` class, which can be obtained using the `getReportingMode()` method of the Sensor object. Knowing the reporting mode of a sensor can help developers write an efficient logic. Reporting modes can be categorized into following four types:

- **Continuous**: In continuous reporting mode, the sensor events are generated at a constant rate defined by the sampling period. This sampling period is set at the time of registering the listener for the sensor. For example, the sensors using the continuous reporting mode are the accelerometer and gyroscope.

- **On Change**: In the on-change reporting mode, the sensor events are generated only if the measured values have changed from the last known values. For example, sensors using the on-change reporting mode are the step counter, proximity, and heart rate sensors.

- **One Shot**: The one shot reporting mode is based on the fire and forget concept. They are triggered only once in the entire duration of the event. The significant motion sensor uses the one shot reporting mode to notify the event. It is only fired once, when the sensor detects the start of significant motion because of walking, running, or driving.

- **Special Trigger**: The special trigger is fired on each occurrence of a particular event. Upon the detection of an event, the sensor values are generated and passed to the listener. The sampling period is ignored in this case. The step detector sensor is an example of the special trigger reporting mode, which is fired on every step taken.

Dealing with specific sensor configuration

There might be some scenarios in which certain features of your application might depend on a specific sensor, and that sensor is not present on the device. In such cases, a good option would be to either turn off that dependent feature or not allow the user to install the application. Let's explore each option in detail.

Checking the availability of the sensor at runtime

If you have a weather utility app, and it uses the pressure sensor on the phone to check the atmospheric pressure, then it's not a good idea to directly use the sensor. There are many Android phones that don't have a pressure sensor on them. If such cases are not handled properly, your application might even crash, which will be a bad user experience.

It's always recommended to check the availability of a sensor before using it in the application. The following code snippet shows how to check the availability of the sensor:

```
private SensorManager mSensorManager;
...
mSensorManager=
(SensorManager)getSystemService(Context.SENSOR_SERVICE);
if(mSensorManager.getDefaultSensor(Sensor.TYPE_PRESSURE)!=null){
  // Success! There's a pressure sensor.
}else{
  // Failure! No pressure sensor.
}
```

Declaring the sensor as mandatory feature

If measuring atmospheric pressure using the phone pressure sensor is the main feature of your application, then you may not want to support those devices that don't have a pressure sensor in them. The Android platform supports this functionality by declaring uses-feature filters in the AndroidManifest.xml file:

```
<uses-feature android:name="android.hardware.sensor.barometer"
android:required="true" />
```

This code snippet informs the Android platform that the pressure sensor is required for this app to function. Google Play uses this uses-feature to filter out those devices that don't have the pressure sensor in them, and hence your app is only installed on the supported devices. The sensors that are supported by uses-feature are the accelerometer, gyroscope, light, barometer (pressure), compass (geomagnetic field), and proximity sensors.

If your application uses a sensor for some feature, but can still run without that sensor by turning off that feature, then it's advisable to declare the sensor in `uses-feature` but still set the required value to false (`android:required="false"`). This informs the operating system that your application uses that sensor, but it can still function without it. It's the developer's responsibility to check the availability of the sensor at runtime.

Sensor availability based on the Android API level

There is a wide variety of sensors that are supported on Android devices. As Android evolved over a period of time, new sensors were added, and some old, inefficient sensors were removed. With the release of newer versions of Android, they got better and more accurate, and the list of supported sensors got bigger. Most of the apps have to support older versions of Android to target the wider audience. But at the same time, not all sensors are supported by older versions of Android. It's a tradeoff between supporting older versions of Android versus getting to use the latest and more advanced sensors that are only available in newer versions of Android.

The following table provides the sensor availability list based on the Android version and API levels. This table illustrates four major platforms to show availability, as the major changes were made in these four platforms only:

Sensor	Android 6.0 (API Level 23)	Android 4.0 (API Level 14)	Android 2.3 (API Level 9)	Android 2.2 (API Level 8)
Accelerometer	Available	Available	Available	Available
Ambient temperature	Available	Available	NA	NA
Gravity	Available	Available	Available	NA
Gyroscope	Available	Available	Available	NA
Light	Available	Available	Available	Available
Linear acceleration	Available	Available	Available	NA
Magnetic field	Available	Available	Available	Available
Orientation	Deprecated	Deprecated	Deprecated	Deprecated
Pressure	Available	Available	Available	NA

Proximity	Available	Available	Available	Available
Relative humidity	Available	Available	NA	NA
Rotation vector	Available	Available	Available	NA
Step Detector	Available	NA	NA	NA
Step Counter	Available	NA	NA	NA
Temperature	Deprecated	Deprecated	Available	Available

Best practice for accessing sensors

Android devices are manufactured by different **OEMs (Original Equipment Manufactures)** and come with various configurations. Each OEM is free to support its own set of sensors, which again come from different vendors. This creates the problem of device fragmentation. This problem is further complicated by addition and deprecation of sensors with different Android API levels. The following are some best practices that will help you deal with this device fragmentation problem and avoid common pitfalls and mistakes:

- Before using the sensor coordinate system, confirm the default orientation mode of the device and check for the orientation of the x and y axes.
- Check the availability, range, minimum delay, reporting modes, and resolution of the sensor before using it.
- Before selecting the sampling period of any sensor, check for its power consumption. Also, keep your application precision and accuracy needs in mind before deciding the sampling period. It's recommended that you select one of the constants given by the operating system.
- Do not block or do heavy processing on the `OnSensorChanged()` method. Your app might miss callbacks or go into **ANR (Application Not Responding)** mode. The app might even crash in the worst cases if this callback is blocked.
- Every registration of the event listener should be paired with the un-registration of the same listener. This should be done at the right time and place. (More on this, in the next chapter).
- Avoid using deprecated sensors and any of the deprecated APIs.

- Never write any kind of application logic based on the delay between the sensor events. Always use the timestamp from the sensor event to do your time-related calculations.

- If some sensors are mandatory for your application to function, then use the `uses-feature` filter in the `Manifest.xml` file and change the required value to true.
- Check your application and its sensor behavior on more than one device, as the sensor values and range may vary with different devices.

Summary

We looked at the important concepts of sensor, their types, values, and common uses. The best practices discussed in this chapter will save you from common errors and mistakes that developers make while writing the code for sensors. It is advisable that you give a second thought to selecting the right sampling period of a sensor, before using them in your code.

This chapter prepared you to dive deep into the Android world of sensors. In the next chapter, we will take a closer look at the classes, interfaces, and methods for accessing sensors, and we will also start writing the code for sensors.

2
Playing with Sensors

In this chapter, we will learn how to write our first sensor program. We will also understand the various callbacks, and how to use these callbacks in the foreground activity and background service. This chapter will also walk you through a basic algorithm developed using sensor values.

We will cover the following topics in this chapter:

- Understanding various sensor framework callbacks
- Using sensors in the foreground activity
- Listing the available sensors on a device
- Knowing individual sensors' capabilities
- Getting the sensor values and updating the user interface
- Monitoring sensor values in the background service

Understanding the sensor framework callbacks

The two most important callbacks of the sensor framework are the `onSensorChanged()` and `onAccuracyChanged()` methods. In order to write efficient sensor code, it's important to understand when these methods are called, and what processing we can do in them. These callbacks are methods of the `SensorEventListnener` interface, which needs to be implemented in the class where the callbacks are to be received:

`onSensorChanged()` is the first callback and has the following syntax:

```
@Override
  public void onSensorChanged(SensorEvent event) {
    }
```

Depending on the type of reporting mode of the sensor, this method will be called, either at regular frequency (Continuous mode) or whenever there is a change in the value of the sensors from the previously reported value (On the change mode). The `onSensorChanged()` method provides the sensor values inside the `float value[]` array of the `SensorEvent` object. These sensor values are different from the previously reported values. There may be instances where the OS can choose to report sensor values at a different frequency than specified at the time of the registration of the listener. Generally, this happens because the OS is heavily loaded and busy with performing some other, more important, processing tasks:

`onAccuracyChanged()` is the second callback and has the following syntax:

```
@Override
  public void onAccuracyChanged(Sensor sensor, int accuracy) {
    }
```

Whenever the OS chooses to change (increase or decrease) the accuracy of the sensor values, it informs your listener using this callback. In this method call, it sends the new accuracy value (Integer) and the sensor object for which the accuracy has changed. Generally, this change in accuracy happens rarely; only when the OS goes into battery-saver mode or gets involved with important heavy-processing tasks. When the OS gets busy, it reduces the accuracy, and when the OS becomes free, it increases the accuracy.

Seeing the big picture

The following sequence diagram explains the logical steps required by your application to get the values from the sensors:

1. The first step is to instantiate the `SensorManager` class from the system sensor service.
2. The second step is to obtain the required `Sensor` class object from `SensorManager`.
3. The third step is to create the `SensorEventListener` interface for your application. We can implement the `SensorEventListener` interface in activity, service, or any other class, and the chosen one will receive the sensor callbacks.

4. The fourth step is to register the `SensorEventListener` with the `SensorManager` class.

5. In the fifth step, after successful registration, your app will start receiving the `SensorEvent` objects in the `onSensorChanged()` method callback of `SensorEventListener`.

6. In the sixth and last step, your app should unregister the `SensorEventListener` interface with the `SensorManager` class when it doesn't require the sensor data any more.

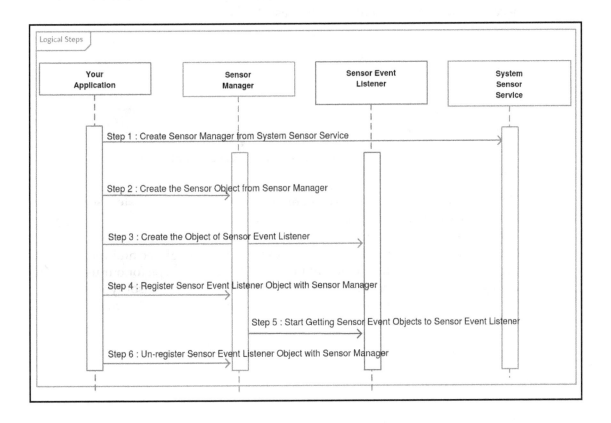

Time for action – using sensors in the foreground activity

In this section, we will explore how to use sensors in the activity. This is the most basic and straightforward way of using sensors. Also, it's the most efficient way if your sensor functionality only ties to that activity:

1. The first step is to implement our activity with the SensorEventListener interface so that our activity can receive SensorEvent through the onSensorChanged() method. The following code snippet shows the necessary import statements and the class declaration:

```
import android.app.Activity;
import android.content.Context;
import android.hardware.Sensor;
import android.hardware.SensorEvent;
import android.hardware.SensorEventListener;
import android.hardware.SensorManager;
import android.os.Bundle;

public class SensorActivity extends Activity implements
SensorEventListener{
```

2. Now, we will create the instance of SensorManager from the system sensor service. The system gives your application a shared instance of SensorManager. The next step is to create the Sensor object from SensorManager. For our example, we will create the object of gyroscope. There might be multiple types of gyroscope sensors on the device, but we need the default type for our use, which is why we use getDefaultSensor() to obtain the default sensor type. We also have to make sure that the Sensor object is not null, meaning that the sensor is actually present on the device:

```
private SensorManager mSensorManager;
private Sensor mSensor;

@Override
protected void onCreate(Bundle savedInstanceState) {
   super.onCreate(savedInstanceState);
   setContentView(R.layout.activity_main);
mSensorManager =
(SensorManager)this.getSystemService
(Context.SENSOR_SERVICE );

if(mSensorManager.getDefaultSensor
```

```
    (Sensor.TYPE_GYROSCOPE) != null){
    mSensor =
    mSensorManager.getDefaultSensor(Sensor.TYPE_GYROSCOPE);
    }
}
```

3. After the creation of the `Sensor` object and `SensorManager`, it's time to register the listener for the callbacks. The registration of the listener is done using the `registerListener()` method of `SensorManager`, which accepts the objects of the `SensorEventListener` interface, the Sensor class, and the sampling period. As a best practice, we should register the listener in the `onResume()` method, and unregister it in the `onPause()` method. By doing this, every time your app goes into the foreground, it will start getting the sensor values, and whenever the app goes into the background, it will stop receiving the sensor values. This will avoid the wastage of the sensor callbacks and hence will save CPU cycles and battery. We also make the `Sensor` and `SensorManager` null in the `onDestroy()` method as a best practice for garbage collection:

```
@Override
protected void onResume() {
    super.onResume();
    mSensorManager.registerListener(this, mSensor,
    SensorManager.SENSOR_DELAY_NORMAL);
}

@Override
protected void onPause() {
    super.onPause();
    mSensorManager.unregisterListener(this);
}

@Override
protected void onDestroy() {
    super.onDestroy();
    mSensorManager = null;
    mSensor = null;
}
```

4. Now, let's talk about the callbacks, where your app will receive the sensor values. The `onSensorChanged()` method is the main callback of the `SenorEventListener` interface, which passes the sensor values in the form of the `SensorEvent` object. The `onAccuracyChanged()` method is the second method that gets called whenever there is a change in the accuracy of the sensor values:

```
@Override
public void onSensorChanged(SensorEvent event) {
    //event.values[] (do something with sensor values)
    //event.timestamp (do something with timestamp)
}

@Override
public void onAccuracyChanged(Sensor sensor, int
accuracy)
{
    //Do something with changed accuracy
    //This method is mandatory to defined
}
```

What just happened?

We just created our first activity with `SenorManager` and `Sensor` objects. We also registered and unregistered listeners. In the coming sections, we will learn how to use sensor callbacks to process the sensor values. This type of code structure is suggested when your sensor scope is limited to one activity only.

Time for action – listing the available sensors on a device

There are multiple sensors available on a device. In this section, we will learn how to get a list of all the available sensors. We will be populating the names of the available sensors in a list and will be displaying it on the screen using `ListView`.

1. The following code block shows the declarations required by the activity. We don't need the `SensorEventListener` interface, as we will not be dealing with the values of the sensor. We declare `ListView`, `ListAdapter`, and `SensorManager`, along with the list of `Sensor` Objects to populate the list:

   ```
   public class SensorListActivity extends Activity
   implements OnItemClickListener{

       private SensorManager mSensorManager;
       private ListView mSensorListView;
       private ListAdapter mListAdapter;
       private List<Sensor> mSensorsList;
   ```

2. In the `onCreate()` method, we instantiate our `SensorManager`, `ListView`, and `ListAdaptor`objects. We will also set the item click listener on our `ListView` and populate the sensor list using the `getSensorList()` method of `SensorManager`, which gives all the available sensors on the device:

   ```
   @Override
   protected void onCreate(Bundle savedInstanceState) {
     super.onCreate(savedInstanceState);
     setContentView(R.layout.activity_main);

     mSensorManager =
     (SensorManager)this.getSystemService
     (Context.SENSOR_SERVICE);

     mSensorsList =
     mSensorManager.getSensorList(Sensor.TYPE_ALL);
     mSensorListView =
     (ListView)findViewById(R.id.session_list);
     mListAdapter = new ListAdapter();
     mSensorListView.setAdapter(mListAdapter);
     mSensorListView.setOnItemClickListener(this);
   }
   ```

3. Now, in the sensor list, we have all the available sensor objects. We will use the same sensor list to inflate our individual `ListView` items. The sensor object has a `getName()` method, which gives the official name of the sensor. We will use the same name to show in our list items. The following `ListAdapter` implementation shows how we use the sensor object list to get the total count and inflate the individual items from the `getName()` method:

```
private class ListAdapter extends BaseAdapter{

private TextView mSensorName;

@Override
public int getCount() {
   return mSensorsList.size();
}

@Override
public Object getItem(int position) {
   return mSensorsList.get(position).getName();
}

@Override
public long getItemId(int position) {
   return position;
}

@Override
public View getView(int position, View convertView,
ViewGroup parent) {

if(convertView==null){
   convertView =
   getLayoutInflater().inflate(R.layout.list_rows,
   parent, false);
}

mSensorName =
(TextView)convertView.findViewById(R.id.sensor_name);
mSensorName.setText(mSensorsList.get(position)
.getName());
return convertView;
  }
}
```

4. The following code block shows the `onItemClick` listener for `ListView`, which we will use for our next example. From this, we take the user to a new `SensorCapabilityActivity`, which will show all the individual sensor details. We pass the sensor type to the next activity so that it can identify the right sensor type:

```
@Override
public void onItemClick(AdapterView<?> parent, View view,
int position,long id) {
    Intent intent = new Intent(getApplicationContext(),
    SensorCapabilityActivity.class);
    intent.putExtra(getResources()
    .getResourceName(R.string.sensor_type),
    mSensorsList.get(position).getType());
    startActivity(intent);
}
```

What just happened?

We populated `ListView` with all the available sensor names on the device. We also used the `getSensorList()` method to get all the sensors, and the `getName()` method to get the official names of the sensors. You will get different names on different devices, depending on the device's OEM implementation. Here is a screenshot of the layout file showing the available sensors on the Nexus 5P device:

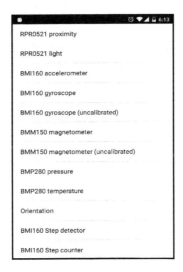

Time for action – knowing individual sensors' capabilities

Android phones are manufactured by different OEMs, which use different vendors to get their sensors. It is very much possible that two different Android phones have different gyroscope sensors, which will have different ranges and other properties. Before developing a universal logic based on sensors, it's important to keep in mind sensor's individual properties and capabilities, which may vary from device to device. In this section, we will explore the common methods for finding out the properties and capabilities of a sensor:

1. We will show the sensor properties in the individual TextView on the screen. In the following code snippet, the TextView, Sensor, and SensorManager variables are declared:

```
public class SensorCapabilityActivity extends Activity {

    private SensorManager mSensorManager;
    private int mSensorType;
    private Sensor mSensor;
    private TextView mSensorNameTextView;
    private TextView mSensorMaximumRangeTextView;
    private TextView mSensorMinDelayTextView;
    private TextView mSensorPowerTextView;
    private TextView mSensorResolutionTextView;
    private TextView mSensorVendorTextView;
    private TextView mSensorVersionTextView;
```

2. In the OnCreated() method, we instantiate the TextView, Sensor, and SensorManager objects. We use the following sensor methods (getName(), getMaximumRange(), getMinDelay(), getPower(), getResolution(), getVendor(), and getVersion()) of the Sensor object to get sensor properties and show the values in their respective TextView. We receive the sensor type through the getIntExtra() API of intent from the previous SensorListActivity:

```
@Override
protected void onCreate(Bundle savedInstanceState) {
    super.onCreate(savedInstanceState);
    setContentView(R.layout.capability_layout);
    Intent intent = getIntent();
```

```
mSensorType = intent.getIntExtra(getResources()
.getResourceName(R.string.sensor_type), 0);
mSensorManager = (SensorManager)this.getSystemService
(Context.SENSOR_SERVICE);
mSensor =
mSensorManager.getDefaultSensor(mSensorType);
mSensorNameTextView = (TextView)findViewById
(R.id.sensor_name);
mSensorMaximumRangeTextView = (TextView)findViewById
(R.id.sensor_range);
mSensorMinDelayTextView = (TextView)findViewById
(R.id.sensor_mindelay);
mSensorPowerTextView = (TextView)findViewById
(R.id.sensor_power);
mSensorResolutionTextView = (TextView)findViewById
(R.id.sensor_resolution);
mSensorVendorTextView = (TextView)findViewById
(R.id.sensor_vendor);
mSensorVersionTextView = (TextView)findViewById
(R.id.sensor_version);
mSensorNameTextView.setText(mSensor.getName());
mSensorMaximumRangeTextView.setText(String.valueOf
(mSensor.getMaximumRange()));
mSensorMinDelayTextView.setText(String.valueOf
(mSensor.getMinDelay()));
mSensorPowerTextView.setText(String.valueOf
(mSensor.getPower()));
mSensorResolutionTextView.setText(String.valueOf
(mSensor.getResolution()));
mSensorVendorTextView.setText(String.valueOf
(mSensor.getVendor()));
mSensorVersionTextView.setText(String.valueOf
(mSensor.getVersion()));
}
```

3. After knowing all the sensor properties, we would like to play with the sensor values. The following `onClickSensorValues()` method takes us to the new activity, which will get the values of the sensor, whose properties are shown in this activity. This `onClickSensorValues()` method is a custom method, which is attached to the button on the screen using the XML `onClick` tag. We pass the sensor type to the next activity so that it can identify the right sensor type:

```
public void onClickSensorValues(View v)
{
    Intent intent = new Intent(getApplicationContext(),
    SensorValuesActivity.class);
    intent.putExtra(getResources().getResourceName
    (R.string.sen sor_type), mSensorType);
    startActivity(intent);
}
```

What just happened?

We used the sensor methods (`getName()`, `getMaximumRange()`, `getMinDelay()`, `getPower()`, `getResolution()`, `getVendor()`, `getVersion()`) of the `Sensor` object and displayed the values on the screen. The following screenshot shows the layout file, showing the capabilities of an accelerometer sensor. These values play an important role when you are developing a universal logic, which should work with all types of sensors on different devices:

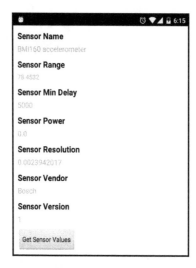

Time for action – getting the sensor values and updating the user interface

Now, let's deal with the most important aspect of sensors, that is, playing with the sensor values. We have created a common activity and screen that can fit a vast number of values for all sensor types. Sensors can have varied values such as temperature or pressure; a light and proximity sensor may have only one value, while sensors such as magnetometer, accelerometer, gyroscope, linear acceleration, and gravity have the three values in the x, y, and z axes. There are other sensors that can have more than three values, for example, rotational vector, geomagnetic rotational vector, game rotational vector, and un-calibrated gyroscope. All the sensor values are passed in an array called values[], which is part of the SensorEvent object.

1. We have created a generic common SensorValuesActivity to display all the values that are coming from the different sensors. We are using the length of values[] array to determine the number of values given by the sensors. For the declaration, we define a maximum of eight TextView, but we will use the same number of TextView as the number of values for that sensor. We also display the time at which the sensor value was generated and the accuracy given by SensorManager. We get the sensor type from the previous activity example in the form of the intent integer value. The following code snippet shows the declaration and initiation of the variables (TextView, time, accuracy, sensor type, Sensor, and SensorManager):

```
public class SensorValuesActivity extends Activity
implements SensorEventListener{

  private SensorManager mSensorManager;
  private int mSensorType;
  private Sensor mSensor;
  private TextView mEventValue_0;
  private TextView mEventValue_1;
  private TextView mEventValue_2;
  private TextView mEventValue_3;
  private TextView mEventValue_4;
  private TextView mEventValue_5;
  private TextView mEventValue_6;
  private TextView mTime;
  private TextView mAccuracy;

  @Override
  protected void onCreate(Bundle savedInstanceState) {
    super.onCreate(savedInstanceState);
```

```
setContentView(R.layout.values_layout);
Intent intent = getIntent();
mSensorType =
intent.getIntExtra(getResources().getResourceName
(R.string.sensor_type), 0);
mSensorManager =
(SensorManager)this.getSystemService
(Context.SENSOR_SERVICE);
mSensor =
mSensorManager.getDefaultSensor(mSensorType;
mEventValue_0 =
(TextView)findViewById(R.id.event0);
mEventValue_1 = (TextView)findViewById(R.id.event1);
mEventValue_2 = (TextView)findViewById(R.id.event2);
mEventValue_3 = (TextView)findViewById(R.id.event3);
mEventValue_4 = (TextView)findViewById(R.id.event4);
mEventValue_5 = (TextView)findViewById(R.id.event5);
mEventValue_6 = (TextView)findViewById(R.id.event6);
mTime = (TextView)findViewById(R.id.time);
mAccuracy = (TextView)findViewById(R.id.accuracy);
}
```

2. As a best practice, we register and unregister the listener for the sensors in the onResume() and onPause() methods, so that we only get the values when the activity is in the foreground:

```
@Override
protected void onResume() {
  super.onResume();
  mSensorManager.registerListener(this, mSensor,
  SensorManager.SENSOR_DELAY_NORMAL);
}

@Override
protected void onPause() {
  super.onPause();
  mSensorManager.unregisterListener(this);
}
```

3. We use the same `onSensorChange()` method to display the sensor values coming from different types of sensor. The length of the `values[]` array is used to determine the number of values for that sensor, and it is also used in setting these sensor values into the same number of `TextView`. We also display the time and accuracy given by the `SensorEvent` object on the screen. In the following code, we set the first `value[0]` without checking, because we are sure that the `SensorEvent` object value's array will have at least one value:

```
@Override
public void onSensorChanged(SensorEvent event) {
  mEventValue_0.setText(String.valueOf
  (event.values[0]));
  mAccuracy.setText(String.valueOf(event.accuracy));
  mTime.setText(String.valueOf(event.timestamp));
  if(event.values.length>1) {
    mEventValue_1.setText(String.valueOf
    (event.values[1]));
  } if(event.values.length>2) {
    mEventValue_2.setText(String.valueOf
    (event.values[2]));
  } if(event.values.length>3) {
    mEventValue_3.setText(String.valueOf
    (event.values[3]));
  } if(event.values.length>4) {
    mEventValue_4.setText(String.valueOf
    (event.values[4]));
  } if(event.values.length>5) {
    mEventValue_5.setText(String.valueOf
    (event.values[5]));
  } if(event.values.length>6) {
    mEventValue_6.setText(String.valueOf
    (event.values[6]));
  }
}
```

What just happened?

We created a common activity to display the different sensors' values on the screen. We used the length of the `values[]` array to get the total number of sensor values and to dynamically set the values in `TextView`. When displaying the sensor values on the UI screen, we should keep in mind the delay between the sensor callbacks. If the delay is very small, that is, 20,000 microseconds or less, then on lower processor devices, the activity UI thread might not be able to update all the sensor values with such a high frequency. Here is a screenshot of the magnetometer values. The first three values are un-calibrated and the next three values are calibrated:

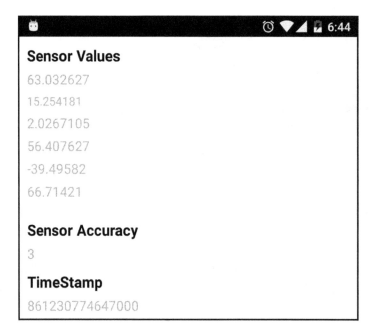

Time for action – processing the sensor values in the background service

There will be cases where your app needs to listen and process the sensor values in the background. Such cases cannot be handled using the activity code structure. We need to use the Android service to handle background sensor processing. Let's discuss the background processing scenario with an example.

The phone handling algorithm

In our example, we will be playing a small MP3 sound when somebody picks up or handles the phone. We will call this event the **phone handling event**, and we will use the Android background service to continuously process the gyroscope sensor values to detect this phone-handling event. The gyroscope gives the rate of rotation of the phone in each x, y, and z axis. When your phone is kept still, there is no, or a very low rate of rotation reported as a value by gyroscope, but when the phone is picked up or handled, the value of rate of rotation goes very high. We will use this logic to define our phone handling event. To consider the rotation in all three axes, we would take the square of the x, y, and z axes, values and then do a square root of it. This would give the magnitude of the vector representing the rate of rotation, and it should be good for our phone handling event detection. If this computed value crosses a particular threshold (in our case, 2.5), then we will call this event a phone handling event". The gyroscope sensor values are reported in radians per second. The threshold of 2.5 is obtained from experimental data. Any movement of the phone by hand always registers a value of more than 2.5 radians per second:

1. We will start by creating the service and initializing the required variables. Our service implements the `SensorEventListener` interface so that it can receive the sensor callbacks. The following is the declaration code for our service class:

```
public class SensorService extends Service implements
SensorEventListener{

    private SensorManager mSensorManager;
    private Sensor mSensor;
    private MediaPlayer mMediaPlayer;
    private boolean isPlaying = false;
    private float mThreshold = 2.5f;
```

2. We will be using the service onCreate() method to initialize our variables. SensorManager and the Sensor object are initialized in the conventional way, as in the activity. We also initialized the MediaPlayer object with a small MP3 sound, which will be played when the phone-handling event triggers. We have used a combination of OnCompletionListener on MediaPlayer and a Boolean isPlaying to make sure that a new instance of MP3 is not played until the previous instance of MP3 has finished playing. When the MP3 has finished playing, we change the isPlaying Boolean to false, and while it's playing, we change isPlaying to true. We only trigger the event when the isPlaying Boolean is true. The MP3 sound file (mario.mp3) is placed in the raw folder created inside the res folder of the project structure:

```
@Override
public void onCreate() {
  super.onCreate();
  mSensorManager =
  (SensorManager)this.getSystemService
  (Context.SENSOR_SERVICE);
  mSensor = mSensorManager.getDefaultSensor
  (Sensor.TYPE_GYROSCOPE);
  mMediaPlayer = MediaPlayer.create
  (getApplicationContext(), R.raw.mario);
  mMediaPlayer.setOnCompletionListener
  (new OnCompletionListener(){
    @Override
    public void onCompletion(MediaPlayer mp) {
    isPlaying = false;
    }
  });
}
```

3. Registering and unregistering listeners is done at different places in the service when compared with activity. In the service, we register the listener in the onStartCommand() method, which is the time when the OS actually starts the service in the background. Similarly, we unregister the listener in the onDestroy() method when the OS kills the service:

```
@Override
public int onStartCommand(Intent intent, int flags,
int startId) {
  mSensorManager.registerListener(this, mSensor,
  SensorManager.SENSOR_DELAY_UI);
  return Service.START_NOT_STICKY;
}
```

```
@Override
public void onDestroy() {
  super.onDestroy();
  mSensorManager.unregisterListener(this);
}
```

4. The core logic of the phone-handling algorithm is written in
   the `onSensorChanged()` method. For each sensor value of the gyroscope, we
   apply this basic algorithm. We calculate the square of each *x*, *y*, and *z* axis value
   by using the standard math power function, and then after summing up the three
   values, we calculate the square root of the summation. The `Math.pow()`
   and `Math.sqrt()` methods are standard Java methods that are part of the
   Android math libraries. The value obtained after this calculation is compared
   with our threshold value, and if it exceeds the threshold, then the MP3 is played
   and we consider this event as a phone handling event. We only play the MP3 if
   it's not already being played. We do this extra check by maintaining the state of
   the `isPlaying` Boolean variable. This check is necessary because the sensor
   values are being processed at a very high frequency, and there is a very high
   chance of crossing the threshold value again before the old MP3 has completed
   playing:

```
@Override
public void onSensorChanged(SensorEvent event) {
  double rateOfRotation =
  Math.sqrt(Math.pow(event.values[0],2) +
  Math.pow(event.values[1], 2) +
  Math.pow(event.values[2], 2));
  if(rateOfRotation>mThreshold){
    if(!isPlaying){
      mMediaPlayer.start();
      isPlaying = true;
    }
  }
}
```

What just happened?

We just created a basic sensor algorithm to detect the phone handling event by processing the gyroscope values in the background service. As a best practice, it's suggested that you don't not block the onSensorChanged() method. In our onSensorChanged() method callback, we are just doing very simple calculations that will be completed before the next callback arrives. If you have any doubt in about whether it's a simple calculation or a complex one, then the best way is to log the time before and after the calculation, and compare it with the time interval between the callbacks.

Summary

We looked at the sensor initialization cycle, important callbacks, and common ways of using the sensors in an activity and a background service. It is advisable to look at the sensors' properties and capabilities before writing a universal logic that will work with all types of sensor on different devices. We also learned about the sensor processing in the background and developed our first sensor algorithm.

In the next chapter, we will extend our understanding by developing a real-world application with the use of different types of sensor. We will also take a closer look at how we can use the sensor values to derive some more useful data.

3

The Environmental Sensors – The Weather Utility App

In this chapter, we will learn how to make use of different types of sensors in our weather utility application. We will also look at how the temperature, relative humidity, and pressure sensor values can be extended to get more useful data such as the altitude, dew point, and absolute humidity. We will explore an alternate source for getting the temperature, relative humidity, and pressure values to compensate for the unavailability of any environment sensor on the phone.

The things you will learn in the this chapter are as follows:

- Understanding the requirements for the weather utility app
- Understanding environmental sensors (temperature, humidity, and pressure)
- How to use the temperature sensor of the phone
- Getting pressure sensor values and calculating the altitude using them
- Getting the relative humidity from the phone sensor and calculating the dew point and absolute humidity using the relative humidity and temperature sensor.
- Comparing the temperature, relative humidity, and pressure values from Web services to phone sensors.

The weather utility app's requirements

Today's Android phones come with environment sensors in them. We will be using the same environment sensors to develop a weather utility app as a part of this chapter. Our app will make use of some additional inputs from external web services combined with our environment sensor's data to drive some more meaningful information, such as dew point, absolute humidity, and altitude. We will also compare weather data obtained from environment sensors to weather data obtained from an external web service. The following are high-level requirements for weather utility apps. The source code of this weather utility app can be found in GitHub under the author's account name and on the support page for the book:

1. Get the outside temperature using the phone's temperature sensor.
2. Get the air pressure using the phone's pressure sensor.
3. Calculate the altitude using the phone's pressure sensor.
4. Get the relative humidity using the phone's humidity sensor.
5. Calculate the dew point and absolute humidity using the temperature and relative humidity sensors in the phone.
6. Using the current phone location, get all the weather data (temperature, pressure, and relative humidity) from the web service (`http://openweathermap.org/api`).
7. Compare the phone environment sensor's data to weather data obtained from The Web service.

Understanding environmental sensors

Environment-based sensors measure environmental conditions (temperature, humidity, and pressure) around the phone and report values only in one dimension (only one value in the `values[]` array). Temperature and humidity sensors have an on-change reporting mode, that is, they will report values whenever there is a change in values from the last reported values, whereas the pressure sensor has a continuous reporting mode; that is, it will report values continuously as per the suggested time interval. Environmental sensors are hardware-based and are only available if a device manufacturer has built them into a device. Because of this, it's particularly important that you verify, at runtime, that an environment sensor exists before you attempt to acquire data from it. Also, unlike motion sensors and position sensors, which often require high-pass or low-pass filtering, environment sensors do not typically require any data filtering or data processing:

- **The temperature sensor**: This measures the ambient air temperature around the phone in degrees Celsius. The string type constant for this sensor is `TYPE_AMBIENT_TEMPERATURE`. There is another type of temperature sensor found on Android devices that measures the device temperature. This device temperature has been deprecated from Android 4.0 (API Level 14) and the string type constant for this sensor is `TYPE_TEMPERATURE`. It's recommended that you not use this device temperature, as some phone manufacturers might not support it.

- **The humidity sensor**: This measures the ambient relative humidity around the phone as a percentage. It is also referred to as relative humidity.
- **The pressure sensor**: It measures ambient air pressure around the phone in mbar (which is also equal to hPa). It is also called a barometer.

There are two more sensors that come under the category of environmental sensors. The first sensor is the device temperature sensor; it measure the temperature of the device in Celsius. This sensor has been deprecated from Android 4.0 (API Level 14). The second sensor is the light sensor, which measures the light illumination in lux. We will discuss the light sensor in the next chapter.

Time for action – using the temperature sensor

In this section, we will get the ambient temperature from the phone temperature sensor and will show it in the foreground activity. Before accessing the value for ambient temperature, we will also check the availability of the temperature sensor on the device.

1. We created a TemperatureActivity and implemented it with the SensorEventListener interface so that it receives the ambient temperature values. We are also checking if the ambient temperature is available on the device and are maintaining the availability state using the isSensorPresent Boolean variable. If the temperature sensor is not present, then we show the relevant message using TextView. The following code snippet shows the necessary steps:

```
public class TemperatureActivity extends Activity
implements SensorEventListener{

  private SensorManager mSensorManager;
  private Sensor mSensor;
  private boolean isSensorPresent;
  private TextView mTemperatureValue;

  @Override
  protected void onCreate(Bundle savedInstanceState) {
    super.onCreate(savedInstanceState);
    setContentView(R.layout.activity_main);
    mSensorManager =
    (SensorManager)this.getSystemService
    (Context.SENSOR_SERVICE);
    mTemperatureValue =
    (TextView)findViewById(R.id.temperaturetext);

    if(mSensorManager.getDefaultSensor
    (Sensor.TYPE_AMBIENT_TEMPERATURE) != null) {
      mSensor = mSensorManager.getDefaultSensor
      (Sensor.TYPE_AMBIENT_TEMPERATURE);
      isSensorPresent = true;
    } else {
      mTemperatureValue.setText("Ambient Temperature
      Sensor is not available!");
      isSensorPresent = false;
    }
  }
}
```

2. We only register and unregister the listener if the temperature sensor is present on the device; we do this using the `isSensorPresent` Boolean variable state. If the temperature sensor is present, then we set the value of ambient temperature in `TextView` inside the `onSensorChanged()` method callback:

```
@Override
protected void onResume() {
  super.onResume();
  if(isSensorPresent) {
    mSensorManager.registerListener(this, mSensor,
    SensorManager.SENSOR_DELAY_NORMAL);
  }
}
@Override
protected void onPause() {
  super.onPause();
  if(isSensorPresent) {
    mSensorManager.unregisterListener(this);
  }
}
@Override
public void onSensorChanged(SensorEvent event) {
  mTemperatureValue.setText("Temperature in degree
  Celsius is " + event.values[0]);
}
```

What just happened?

We created temperature activity with the `SenorManager` and `Sensor` objects. We also registered and unregistered listeners, depending on the availability of the temperature sensor. After receiving the temperature value in the `onSensorChanged()` method, we updated `TextView` with this value.

Getting air pressure from the phone's pressure sensor

The procedure to get values from the phone's pressure sensor is exactly the same as the previous example showing getting values from temperature sensors. The only difference is the sensor type. To get values from the pressure sensor, we have to specify the sensor type as `TYPE_PRESSURE`. All other best practices (initiating `SensorManager`, the `Sensor` object, and registering and unregistering the listener and sensor callback) remain the same as they were in the previous temperature sensor example.

Time for action – calculating the altitude using the pressure sensor

Once we have atmospheric pressure from the phone's pressure sensor, we can calculate the altitude of the phone using the `getAltitude(float p0, float p1)` method of the `SensorManager` class. The first parameter of the altitude API is the atmospheric pressure at sea level, and the second parameter is the atmospheric pressure of the current location, which can be obtained from the phone's pressure sensor. To get a more accurate altitude value, the exact atmospheric pressure at sea level should be obtained from any third-party service such as an airport database.

If the exact atmospheric pressure at sea level is not available, then in its place we can use the standard atmospheric pressure given by the `SensorManager` class, `PRESSURE_STANDARD_ATMOSPHERE`. This will give a good approximate altitude value. In this section, we will walk you through the steps of calculating the altitude using the phone's pressure sensor:

1. We created a `PressureAltitudeActivity` and followed the usual steps showing getting values from the sensor, which are implementing the `SensorEventListener` interface, initiating the `SensorManager` and `Sensor` object, and checking the availability of sensors. The following code snippet shows the necessary steps:

   ```
   public class PressureAltitudeActivity extends Activity
   implements SensorEventListener{
     private SensorManager mSensorManager;
     private Sensor mSensor;
     private boolean isSensorPresent;
     private TextView mPressureValue;
     private TextView mAltitudeValue;
   ```

```
@Override
protected void onCreate(Bundle savedInstanceState) {
  super.onCreate(savedInstanceState);
  setContentView(R.layout.pressurealtitude_layout);
  mPressureValue =
  (TextView)findViewById(R.id.pressuretext);
  mAltitudeValue =
  (TextView)findViewById(R.id.altitudetext);
  mSensorManager = (SensorManager)
  this.getSystemService(Context.SENSOR_SERVICE);
  if(mSensorManager.getDefaultSensor
  (Sensor.TYPE_PRESSURE) != null) {
    mSensor = mSensorManager.getDefaultSensor
    (Sensor.TYPE_PRESSURE);
    isSensorPresent = true;
  } else {
   isSensorPresent = false;
   mPressureValue.setText("Pressure Sensor is not
   available!");
   mAltitudeValue.setText("Cannot calculate
   altitude, as pressure Sensor is not available!");
  }
}
```

2. After the registering and unregistering of the listener, we calculate altitude using the `SensorManager.getAltitude(pressure01,pressure02)` method, in which we pass the standard air pressure as a first argument, after which we pass the current air pressure obtained from the phone's pressure sensor as a second argument. This gives us the altitude of that particular place:

```
@Override
protected void onResume() {
  super.onResume();
  if(isSensorPresent) {
    mSensorManager.registerListener(this, mSensor,
    SensorManager.SENSOR_DELAY_NORMAL);
  }
}

@Override
protected void onPause() {
  super.onPause();
  if(isSensorPresent) {
    mSensorManager.unregisterListener(this);
  }
}
```

```
@Override
public void onSensorChanged(SensorEvent event) {
    float pressure = event.values[0];
    mPressureValue.setText("Pressure in mbar is " +
    pressure);
    float altitude = SensorManager.getAltitude
    (SensorManager.PRESSURE_STANDARD_ATMOSPHERE,
    pressure);
    mAltitudeValue.setText("Current altitude is " +
    altitude);
}
```

What just happened?

We just calculated the altitude of a particular place using the air pressure of that place and the standard sea-level air pressure. We did this using the `SensorManager.getAltitude(pressure01,pressure02)` method. We can increase the accuracy of the altitude calculation by supplying the exact sea-level air pressure instead of using the standard sea-level air pressure given by `SensorManager`. The exact sea-level air pressure can be obtained from many online web services, such as `http://www.worldweat heronline.com/api/marine-weather-api.aspx`.

Getting relative humidity from the phone's humidity sensor

Getting values from the phone's relative humidity sensor is a very similar process to getting values from the temperature or pressure sensors. The only difference is in specifying the sensor type. To get the values from the relative humidity sensor, we have to specify the sensor type as `TYPE_RELATIVE_HUMIDITY`. All the other standard practices (initiating `SensorManager`, the `Sensor` object, and registering and unregistering the listener and the sensor callback) remain the same. Another point to note is that *humidity* and *relative humidity* are used interchangeably; they both refer to the same value.

Time for action – calculating the dew point and absolute humidity

We can use the phone's relative humidity and temperature sensor to calculate the dew point and absolute humidity. Before calculating, let's look at the definition and formula of the dew point and absolute humidity.

- **Dew Point**: The dew point is the temperature at which a given volume of air must be cooled, at constant barometric pressure, for water vapor to condense into water. The following equation shows how you can calculate the dew point using the temperature and relative humidity. The derivation and analysis of this formula are beyond the scope this book:

$$Td = Tn * \frac{ln(Rh/100\%) + m*Tc/(Tn+Tc)}{m - [ln(Rh/100\%) + m*Tc/(Tn+Tc)]}$$

Let's look at what each term represents:

- Td is the dew point temperature in degrees C
- Tc is the current temperature in degrees C from the phone' sensor
- Rh is the actual relative humidity as a percentage (%) from the phone's sensor
- m is 17.62 (the mass constant)
- Tn is 243.12 (the temperature constant)

- **Absolute Humidity**: The absolute humidity is the mass of water vapor in a given volume of dry air. Absolute humidity is measured in grams/cubic meters. The following equation shows how you can calculate absolute humidity using temperature and relative humidity. The derivation and analysis of this formula are also beyond the scope of this book:

$$Dv = Ta * \frac{(Rh/100\%)*A* exp(m*Tc/(Tn+Tc)}{K+Tc}$$

Let's look at what each term represents:

- Dv is the absolute humidity in grams/meter^3
- Tc is the current temperature in degrees C from the phone's sensor
- Rh is the actual relative humidity as a percentage (%) from the phone's sensor
- m is 17.62 (the mass constant)
- Tn is 243.12 (the temperature constant)
- A is 6.112 hPa (the pressure constant)
- K is 273.15 (the Kelvin constant)
- Ta is 216.7 (the temperature constant)

Let's look at the implementation of these formulae to calculate the dew point and absolute humidity using the phone's temperature and relative humidity sensors.

1. We have created a `HumidityActivity` and followed the standard steps of getting values from the sensor, which are implementing the `SensorEventListener` interface, and initiating the `SensorManager` and `Sensor` Objects for relative humidity and temperature sensors. Both the relative humidity and temperature sensors are mandatory for calculating the dew point and absolute humidity; if they are not present, then we show the user the appropriate message. The following code snippet demonstrates the necessary steps:

```
public class HumidityActivity extends Activity
implements SensorEventListener {

    private SensorManager mSensorManager;
    private Sensor mHumiditySensor;
    private Sensor mTemperatureSensor;
    private boolean isHumiditySensorPresent;
    private boolean isTemperatureSensorPresent;
    private TextView mRelativeHumidityValue;
    private TextView mAbsoluteHumidityValue;
    private TextView mDewPointValue;
    private float mLastKnownRelativeHumidity = 0;

    @Override
    protected void onCreate(Bundle savedInstanceState) {
      super.onCreate(savedInstanceState);
      setContentView(R.layout.humidity_layout);
      mRelativeHumidityValue =
      (TextView)findViewById(R.id.relativehumiditytext);
      mAbsoluteHumidityValue =
```

```
(TextView)findViewById(R.id.absolutehumiditytext);
mDewPointValue =
(TextView)findViewById(R.id.dewpointtext);
mSensorManager = (SensorManager)
this.getSystemService(Context.SENSOR_SERVICE);

if(mSensorManager.getDefaultSensor
(Sensor.TYPE_RELATIVE_HUMIDITY) != null) {
  mHumiditySensor = mSensorManager.getDefaultSensor
  (Sensor.TYPE_RELATIVE_HUMIDITY);
  isHumiditySensorPresent = true;
}
else {
  mRelativeHumidityValue.setText("Relative Humidity
  Sensor is not available!");
  mAbsoluteHumidityValue.setText("Cannot calculate
  Absolute Humidity, as relative humidity sensor is
  not available!");
  mDewPointValue.setText("Cannot calculate Dew
  Point, as relative humidity sensor is not
  available!");
  isHumiditySensorPresent = false;
}

if(mSensorManager.getDefaultSensor
(Sensor.TYPE_AMBIENT_TEMPERATURE) != null) {
  mTemperatureSensor =
  mSensorManager.getDefaultSensor
  (Sensor.TYPE_AMBIENT_TEMPERATURE);
  isTemperatureSensorPresent = true;
} else {
  mAbsoluteHumidityValue.setText("Cannot calculate
  Absolute Humidity, as temperature sensor is not
  available!");
  mDewPointValue.setText("Cannot calculate Dew
  Point, as temperature sensor is not available!");
  isTemperatureSensorPresent = false;
}
}
```

2. We first register and unregister the listeners in the `onResume()` and `onPause()` methods. We are using the same activity as a listener for both the temperature and relative humidity sensors, and that's why we will get both the sensor values in the same `onSensorChanged()` callback. For every sensor event value, we have to check what kind of sensor value it contains, which can be done using the `sensor.getType()` method on the sensor event value. We show the relative humidity value in `TextView` and store it in the `lastKnownRelativeHumidity` float variable. Once we get the temperature value from the sensor, we pass the `lastKnownRelativeHumidity` value and the temperature value to the `calculateDewPoint(float temperature, float relativeHumidity)` and `calculateAbsoluteHumidity(float temperature, float relativeHumidity)` methods. These methods implement the dew point and absolute humidity formulae discussed previously using the standard Math functions:

```
@Override
public void onSensorChanged(SensorEvent event) {
    if(event.sensor.getType() ==
    Sensor.TYPE_RELATIVE_HUMIDITY) {
        mRelativeHumidityValue.setText("Relative Humidity
        in % is " + event.values[0]);
        mLastKnownRelativeHumidity = event.values[0];
    } else
    if(event.sensor.getType() ==
    Sensor.TYPE_AMBIENT_TEMPERATURE) {
        if(mLastKnownRelativeHumidity !=0) {
            float temperature = event.values[0];
            float absoluteHumidity =
            calculateAbsoluteHumidity(temperature,
            mLastKnownRelativeHumidity);
            mAbsoluteHumidityValue.setText("The absolute
            humidity at temperature: " + temperature + " is: "
            + absoluteHumidity);
            float dewPoint = calculateDewPoint(temperature,
            mLastKnownRelativeHumidity);
            mDewPointValue.setText("The dew point at
            temperature: " + temperature + " is: " +
            dewPoint);
        }
    }
}

/* Meaning of the constants
Dv: Absolute humidity in grams/meter3
m: Mass constant
```

```
Tn: Temperature constant
Ta: Temperature constant
Rh: Actual relative humidity in percent (%) from phone's
sensor
Tc: Current temperature in degrees C from phone' sensor
A: Pressure constant in hP
K: Temperature constant for converting to kelvin
*/
public float calculateAbsoluteHumidity(float
temperature, float relativeHumidity)
{
  float Dv = 0;
  float m = 17.62f;
  float Tn = 243.12f;
  float Ta = 216.7f;
  float Rh = relativeHumidity;
  float Tc = temperature;
  float A = 6.112f;
  float K = 273.15f;
  Dv = (float) (Ta * (Rh/100) * A *
  Math.exp(m*Tc/(Tn+Tc)) / (K + Tc));
  return Dv;
}

/* Meaning of the constants
Td: Dew point temperature in degrees Celsius
m: Mass constant
Tn: Temperature constant
Rh: Actual relative humidity in percent (%) from phone's
sensor
Tc: Current temperature in degrees C from phone' sensor
*/
public float calculateDewPoint(float temperature, float
relativeHumidity)
{
  float Td = 0;
  float m = 17.62f;
  float Tn = 243.12f;
  float Rh = relativeHumidity;
  float Tc = temperature;

  Td = (float) (Tn * ((Math.log(Rh/100) +
  m*Tc/(Tn+Tc))/(m - (Math.log(Rh/100) +
  m*Tc/(Tn+Tc)))));
  return Td;
}
```

What just happened?

We just calculated the dew point and absolute humidity from the temperature and relative humidity values using the standard equations. More details on the constants and equation used in our implementation can be found at `http://goo.gl/OrsFyP` and also in the source code bundle for this chapter, which is available on the support page for the book.

Time for action – comparing the temperature, humidity, and pressure values from web services to phone sensors

In previous sections, we have got the phone's sensor values for temperature, relative humidity, and pressure. There are a lot of Android devices that may not have all three sensors in them, so we want to look at an alternative way to get the temperature, relative humidity, and pressure values using the current location from the phone via a third-party web service. Using the alternative way, we can compare the accuracy of our phone sensor values and it will also compensate for the non-availability of any environmental sensor for our weather utility application.

Third-party web service – open weather map

We will be using a third-party web service from the open weather map. This provides a basic free web service to get the temperature, pressure, and relative humidity values for a particular location. This is a GET RESTful web service, in which we pass the current location co-ordinates in the form of latitude and longitude parameters. It accepts the latitude and longitude in the URL parameters and returns a JSON response containing all the weather information for that particular location. We also have to append units and the app ID in the URL:

1. The following is a sample request for this web service. It accepts four parameters: the latitude and longitude of the current location, units (metric or imperial), and the App ID, which can be generated by registering with an open weather map website (`http://api.openweathermap.org/data/2.5/weather?lat=42.07 1635&lon=-88.0486294&units=metric&APPID=5bcc10ceaffa83dfb77056b 5470b1e46`).

2. The following is the sample JSON response for the preceding request:

```json
{
  "coord": {
    "lon": -88.05,
    "lat": 42.07
  },
  "sys": {
    "message": 0.5879,
    "country": "US",
    "sunrise": 1432462993,
    "sunset": 1432516496
  },
  "weather": [
    {
      "id": 804,
      "main": "Clouds",
      "description": "overcast clouds",
      "icon": "04d"
    }
  ],
  "base": "stations",
  "main": {
    "temp": 22.99,
    "temp_min": 22.99,
    "temp_max": 22.99,
    "pressure": 1006.18,
    "sea_level": 1033.55,
    "grnd_level": 1006.18,
    "humidity": 45
  },
  "wind": {
    "speed": 3.11,
    "deg": 128.501
  },
  "clouds": {
    "all": 92
  },
  "dt": 1432485188,
  "id": 4905211,
  "name": "Palatine",
  "cod": 200
}
```

We will be using the `temp`, `pressure`, and `humidity` values from the JSON response from this web service. Further details of the web service API, request parameters, and response fields can be found at the following link: `http://openweathermap.org/curren t.`

Using Google Play Services Location API and AsyncTask

To get the current location of the phone, we will be using the Google Play services location API. Details can be found in the official documentation at `https://developer.android. com/training/location/retrieve-current.html`. We will also explain the Google Play Services Location API with examples in the bonus chapter, Sensor Fusion and Sensors-Based API – The Driving Event Detection App.

We will be implementing the web service call inside the `WeatherAsyncTask` class, which is extended from the `AsyncTask` class. `AsyncTask` is a utility class provided by the Android framework that allows you to perform background operations and publish the results on the UI thread without having to manipulate threads and handlers. Once we obtain the current location using the Google Play services location API, we will be calling the `openweathermap` web service inside the `WeatherAsyncTask`.

Let's look at the stepwise implementation of the whole process:

1. We created a `CompareSensorActivity` and followed the standard steps for the sensor initiation cycle, which comprises implementing the `SensorEventListener` interface, initiating the `SensorManager` and `Sensor` objects, and checking the availability of individual sensors. We also initialized `TextView` to show the values from the phone's sensors and web service. We implemented the `ConnectionCallbacks` and `OnConnectionFailedListener` interfaces to get the callbacks from the Google play services location API:

```
public class CompareSensorActivity extends Activity
implements SensorEventListener, ConnectionCallbacks,
OnConnectionFailedListener{

  private SensorManager mSensorManager;
  private Sensor mHumiditySensor;
  private Sensor mTemperatureSensor;
  private Sensor mPressureSensor;
  private boolean isHumiditySensorPresent;
```

```
private boolean isTemperatureSensorPresent;
private boolean isPressureSensorPresent;
private TextView mRelativeHumiditySensorValue;
private TextView mPressureSensorValue;
private TextView mTemperatureSensorValue;
private TextView mRelativeHumidityWSValue;
private TextView mPressureWSValue;
private TextView mTemperatureWSValue;
protected GoogleApiClient mGoogleApiClient;
protected Location mLastLocation;


@Override
protected void onCreate(Bundle savedInstanceState) {
 super.onCreate(savedInstanceState);
 setContentView(R.layout.comparesensor_layout);

 mRelativeHumiditySensorValue =
 (TextView)findViewById(R.id.relativehumiditytext);
 mTemperatureSensorValue =
 (TextView)findViewById(R.id.temperaturetext);
 mPressureSensorValue =
 (TextView)findViewById(R.id.pressuretext);
 mRelativeHumidityWSValue =
(TextView)findViewById(R.id.relativehumiditywstext);
mPressureWSValue =
(TextView)findViewById(R.id.pressurewstext);
mTemperatureWSValue =
(TextView)findViewById(R.id.temperaturewstext);
mSensorManager = (SensorManager)
this.getSystemService(Context.SENSOR_SERVICE);
if(mSensorManager.getDefaultSensor
(Sensor.TYPE_RELATIVE_HUMIDITY) != null) {
  mHumiditySensor = mSensorManager.getDefaultSensor
  (Sensor.TYPE_RELATIVE_HUMIDITY);
  isHumiditySensorPresent = true;
} else {
  mRelativeHumiditySensorValue.setText("Relative
  Humidity Sensor is not available!");
  isHumiditySensorPresent = false;
}
if(mSensorManager.getDefaultSensor
(Sensor.TYPE_AMBIENT_TEMPERATURE) != null) {
mTemperatureSensor = mSensorManager.getDefaultSensor
(Sensor.TYPE_AMBIENT_TEMPERATURE);
isTemperatureSensorPresent = true;
} else {
  isTemperatureSensorPresent = false;
```

```
        mTemperatureSensorValue.setText("Temperature
        Sensor is not available!");
    }
    if(mSensorManager.getDefaultSensor
    (Sensor.TYPE_PRESSURE) != null) {
        mPressureSensor = mSensorManager.getDefaultSensor
        (Sensor.TYPE_PRESSURE);
        isPressureSensorPresent = true;
    } else {
        isPressureSensorPresent = false;
        mPressureSensorValue.setText("Pressure Sensor is
        not available!");
    }
    buildGoogleClient();
}
```

2. To get the last known current location, we create the Google API Client object and initialize Google Play services listeners. We request to connect with Google services in the `onStart()` method and disconnect in the `onStop()` method. Once the Google services are connected, we get the `onConnected(Bundle connectionHint)` callback. We use this callback to get the last known location from the `FusedLocationAPI`. After obtaining the location, we create a new object of `WeatherAsyncTask` and start its execution by passing the current location object into it. As a standard practice, we register and unregister the listener for sensors in the `onResume()` and `onPause()` methods:

```
public void buildGoogleClient()
{
    mGoogleApiClient = new
    GoogleApiClient.Builder(this).
    addConnectionCallbacks(this).
    addOnConnectionFailedListener(this).
    addApi(LocationServices.API).build();
}

@Override
public void onConnected(Bundle connectionHint) {
mLastLocation =
LocationServices.FusedLocationApi.getLastLocation
(mGoogleApiClient);
new WeatherAsyncTask().execute(mLastLocation);
}

@Override
protected void onStart() {
    super.onStart();
```

```
    mGoogleApiClient.connect();
  }

  @Override
  protected void onStop() {
    super.onStop();
    if (mGoogleApiClient.isConnected()) {
      mGoogleApiClient.disconnect();
    }
  }
```

3. We use the `onSensorChanged()` method to display phone sensor values in `TextView` coming from different types of sensors. We created the `WeatherAsyncTask` class and extended it from `AsyncTask` to give it lightweight thread functionality. In the `doInBackground(object...params)` method of this class, which is executed in the background thread, we hit the Web service to get temperature, pressure, and relative humidity values. As a first step to hitting the web service, we create the web service request by appending the latitude and longitude in URL parameters, which are obtained by the `FusedLocationAPI`. We also add the app id and unit type as metrics in the URL parameters. The app id values can be obtained from the open weather map website after registering with them. As a second step, with the complete URL parameters, we hit the Web service using the `HttpURLConnection` object. In the third step, we parse the JSON response and extract the temperature, pressure, and humidity values using the `JSONObject` class in temporary variables. Once parsing is successful, we display the temperature, pressure, and humidity values from the web service in `TextView` in the `onPostExecute(String result)` method, which is executed after completing the processing of the `doInBackground(object...params)` method:

```
  @Override
  public void onSensorChanged(SensorEvent event) {
    if(event.sensor.getType() ==
    Sensor.TYPE_RELATIVE_HUMIDITY) {
      mRelativeHumiditySensorValue.setText("Relative
      Humidity from Phone Sensor in % is " +
      event.values[0]);
    } else if(event.sensor.getType() ==
    Sensor.TYPE_AMBIENT_TEMPERATURE) {
      mTemperatureSensorValue.setText("Temperature from
      Phone Sensor in degree Celsius is " +
      event.values[0]);
    } else if(event.sensor.getType() ==
    Sensor.TYPE_PRESSURE) {
      mPressureSensorValue.setText("Pressure from Phone
```

```
      Sensor in mbar is " + event.values[0]);
  }
}

public class WeatherAsyncTask extends
AsyncTask<Object, Void, String>{

  private float mTemperature;
  private float mPressure;
  private float mRelativeHumidity;
  private String mUrlString =
  "http://api.openweathermap.org/data/2.5/weather?";
  private Location mLastKnownLocation;
  private boolean isResponseSuccessful = false;
  private String AppId =
  "5bcc10ceaffa83dfb77056b5470b1e46";//Replace with
  your own AppId

  @Override
  protected void onPostExecute(String result) {
    super.onPostExecute(result);
    if(isResponseSuccessful)
    {
      runOnUiThread(new Runnable() {
        @Override
        public void run() {
          mRelativeHumidityWSValue.setText("Relative
          humidity from Web service in % is " +
          mRelativeHumidity);
          mPressureWSValue.setText("Pressure from Web
          service in mbar is " + mPressure);
          mTemperatureWSValue.setText("Temperature
          from Web service in Celsius is " +
          mTemperature);
        }
      });
    }
  }

  @Override
  protected String doInBackground(Object... params) {
    mLastKnownLocation = (Location)params[0];
    String urlparams = mUrlString +
    "lat="+mLastKnownLocation.getLatitude()
    +"&lon="+mLastKnownLocation.getLongitude()
    +"&units=metric&APPID="+AppId;
    try {
      URL url = new URL(urlparams);
```

```
        HttpURLConnection mHttpURLConnection =
        (HttpURLConnection) url.openConnection();
        mHttpURLConnection.setRequestMethod("GET");
        mHttpURLConnection.connect();
        BufferedReader mBufferedReader = new
        BufferedReader(new InputStreamReader
        (mHttpURLConnection.getInputStream()));
        String inputLine;
        StringBuffer response = new StringBuffer();
        while ((inputLine = mBufferedReader.readLine())
        != null)
        {
          response.append(inputLine);
        }
      mBufferedReader.close();
      mHttpURLConnection.disconnect();
      JSONObject responseObject = new
      JSONObject(response.toString());
      if(!responseObject.isNull("main"))
      {
        JSONObject mainJsonObject =
        responseObject.getJSONObject("main");
        mTemperature = (float)
        mainJsonObject.getDouble("temp");
        mPressure = (float)
        mainJsonObject.getDouble("pressure");
        mRelativeHumidity = (float)
        mainJsonObject.getDouble("humidity");
        isResponseSuccessful = true;
      }
    } catch (Exception e) {
    }
    return null;
  }
}
```

What just happened?

We first obtained the temperature, pressure, and humidity values from the phone's sensor using the standard sensors initialization cycle. Then, we got the same temperature, pressure, and humidity values from the openweathermap web service using the current location from the FusedLocationAPI of the Google Play services. We used the AsyncTask utility to hit the openweathermap web service, and we parsed the JSON response using the JSONObject class. Comparing the temperature, pressure, and humidity values from the openweathermap web service to the phone's sensor gives us a fair idea of the phone sensor's accuracy. Also, the web service's values may compensate for any non-availability of any of the weather-related sensors in the phone. The following screenshot shows the layout file displaying a comparison of the sensor's values with the web service's values on the Nexus 5P device:

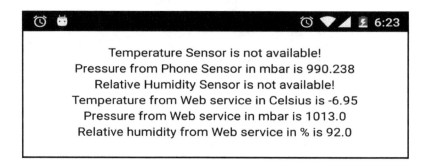

Summary

In this chapter, we learned how to use various environment sensors. We also derived of altitude, absolute humidity, and dew point values using the temperature, pressure, and relative humidity sensors. We also looked at alternate sources (the openweathermap web service) to obtain the temperature, relative humidity, and pressure values to compensate for the non-availability of any environment sensor on the phone.

In the next chapter, we will learn how to use light and proximity sensors, and we will look at how they can be used in real-world applications.

4
The Light and Proximity Sensors

In this chapter, we will learn about proximity and light sensors, and we will develop a small application using them. We will also learn about the concepts of wake locks and wakeup and non-wakeup sensors. We will understand the hardware sensor FIFO queue and what happens to sensors when the application processor goes into suspended mode.

You will learn the following things in this chapter:

- Understanding the light and proximity sensors.
- Understanding requirements for the automatic torchlight and screen brightness app.
- How to use the proximity sensor in the phone and turn phone's flashlight off and on.
- How to use the phone's light sensor and adjust the screen brightness.
- What are wake locks and how should we use them?
- What are wakeup and non-wakeup sensors, and what is the hardware FIFO sensor queue?

Understanding the light and proximity sensors

The light sensor is a part of the environmental sensors, and the proximity sensor is a part of the positional sensors for Android. Both light and proximity sensors can be found in almost every Android device today. The light sensor is responsible for measuring the illuminance in lux. Illuminance is the amount of light striking a surface. It is also known as incident light, where the "incident" is the beam of light actually landing on the surface.

The proximity sensor measures the proximity of any object near the screen. There are two types of proximity sensor found on Android devices.

- The first type of the proximity sensor provides the absolute distance in centimetres between the object and the phone. There are very few phones which support this type of proximity sensor.
- The second type of sensor gives only two values in form of integers, which represents the proximity of the object from the phone. When the object is near, then the value is 0, while when the object is far, then the value is the maximum range of the proximity sensor, which generally lies between 5 to 20 centimeters. For example, the Samsung Galaxy S5 has the far value of 8, while the LG Nexus 5 has the far value of 5.

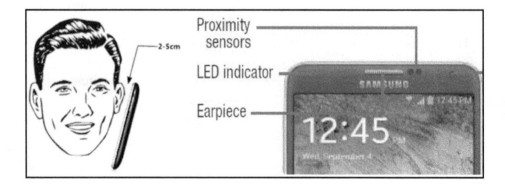

Most Android devices have the same hardware, which works for both light and proximity sensors, but Android still treats them as logically separate sensors. It depends on whether the individual **OEMs** (**Original Equipment Manufactures**) have a single hardware or two separate hardware to support both the logical sensors.

The light and proximity sensor is generally located on the top right-hand section of the phone, a few millimetres to the right of the earpiece. You have to look very carefully to spot the sensor as it's barely visible because of its small size. Generally, it's a pair of small black holes covered under the screen. Some OEMs might choose a different location for the light and proximity sensor, but mostly it will be on the top edge of the phone. For example, Samsung Galaxy S devices have them on the right-hand side of the earpiece, while HTC Android devices have them on the left-hand side of the earpiece.

The automatic torch light and screen brightness app requirements

As a learning assignment for this chapter, we will be developing a small application that will make use of the light and proximity sensor in the phone to turn on and turn off the flash light and adjust the screen brightness. This app will be running in the foreground Android activity and will start processing the sensor values on `onResume()` and will stop on `onPause()`. We will have the separate activity for each proximity sensor and light sensor, and both will work independently. The following are the high-level requirements for the automatic torch light application:

1. Create an Android activity to process the proximity sensor values.
2. Whenever any object comes close to the phone (the proximity sensor gives the near value), turn on the flashlight, and whenever that object goes away from the phone (the proximity sensor gives the far value), then turn off the flashlight.
3. Create an Android activity to process the light sensor values.
4. Whenever the phone enters any dark area, increase the screen brightness of the phone, and when the phone goes back to a lighted area, decrease the screen brightness.

Time for action – turning the torch light on and off using the proximity sensor

In this section, we will be learning how to use the proximity sensor to turn the camera flash light on and off. As discussed earlier, most proximity sensors return the absolute distance in cm, but some return only the near and far values. The near value is 0 and the far value is the maximum range of the proximity sensor. There are a lot of common use cases for proximity sensors, such as to turn off the screen while the user is on a call, or to detect if the phone is inside the pocket or outside. For our example, we will be turning the camera flashlight on whenever any object comes near the phone screen and turning it off when the object goes far from the phone screen. The proximity sensor has on-change reporting mode, the details of reporting modes are explained in Chapter 1, *Sensor Fundamentals*. It is fired as soon as the proximity of the object near the phone changes.

The following code shows how to use the proximity sensor to turn the camera flash light on or off.

1. We created a ProximitySensorActivity and followed the standard steps to get values from the sensor, which are implementing the SensorEventListener interface, initiating the SensorManager and Sensor Objects, and checking the availability of the sensors. We also declared the Camera, SurfaceTexture, and Paramters objects required for the camera flashlight to work. We also called the custom initCameraFlashlight() method from onCreate() to initialize the required camera objects:

```
public class ProximitySensorActivity extends Activity implements
SensorEventListener{

    private SensorManager mSensorManager;
    private Sensor mSensor;
    private boolean isSensorPresent;
    private float distanceFromPhone;
    private Camera mCamera;
    private SurfaceTexture mPreviewTexture;
    private Camera.Parameters mParameters;
    private boolean isFlashLightOn = false;

    protected void onCreate(Bundle savedInstanceState) {
        super.onCreate(savedInstanceState);
        setContentView(R.layout.proximitysensor_layout);
        mSensorManager = (SensorManager)this.getSystemService
        (Context.SENSOR_SERVICE);
        if(mSensorManager.getDefaultSensor(Sensor.TYPE_PROXIMITY)
```

```
      != null) {
        mSensor = mSensorManager.getDefaultSensor
        (Sensor.TYPE_PROXIMITY);
        isSensorPresent = true;
      } else {
        isSensorPresent = false;
      }

      initCameraFlashLight();
    }
```

2. As a best practice, we registered the listener in the `onResume()` method and un-registered it in the `onPause()` method. Inside the custom `initCameraFlashlight()` method, we initialized the `Camera`, `SurfaceTexture`, and `Paramters` objects required for turning on the flashlight. In the `onDestroy()` method of the activity, we released the `Camera` object and set all the initialized object references to null:

```
@Override
protected void onResume() {
  super.onResume();
  if(isSensorPresent) {
    mSensorManager.registerListener(this, mSensor,
    SensorManager.SENSOR_DELAY_NORMAL);
  }
}

@Override
protected void onPause() {
  super.onPause();
  if(isSensorPresent) {
    mSensorManager.unregisterListener(this);
  }
}

public void initCameraFlashLight()
{
  mCamera = Camera.open();
  mParameters = mCamera.getParameters();
  mPreviewTexture = new SurfaceTexture(0);
  try {
    mCamera.setPreviewTexture(mPreviewTexture);
  } catch (IOException ex) {
      Log.e(TAG, ex.getLocalizedMessage());
      Toast.makeText(getApplicationContext(),
      getResources().getText(R.string.error_message),
      Toast.LENGTH_SHORT).show();
```

```
        }
    }

    @Override
    protected void onDestroy() {
        super.onDestroy();
        mSensorManager = null;
        mSensor = null;
        mCamera.release();
        mCamera = null;
    }
}
```

3. After initiating `SurfaceTexture`, camera, and sensors, we will now write our core logic for the app. In our custom `turnTorchLightOn()` method, we start the flash light by setting the flash mode to `FLASH_MODE_TORCH` for the camera parameters and starting the camera preview. Similarly, in the custom `turnTorchLightOff()` method, we stop the flash light by setting the flash mode to `FLASH_MODE_OFF` for the camera parameters and stopping the camera preview. Now, we call these methods from the `onSensorChanged()` method, depending on the distance of any object from the proximity sensor. If the distance of any object from the phone's proximity sensor is less than the maximum range of the proximity sensor, then we consider the object to be near and call the custom `turnTorchLighOn()` method; however, if the distance is equal to or greater than the range of the proximity sensor, we consider the object is far and call the `turnTorchLightOff()` method. We use the `isFlashLightOn` Boolean variable to maintain the on/off states of the flashlight:

```
public void turnTorchLightOn()
{
    mParameters.setFlashMode(Camera.Parameters.FLASH_MODE_TORCH);
    mCamera.setParameters(mParameters);
    mCamera.startPreview();
    isFlashLightOn = true;
}

public void turnTorchLightOff()
{
    mParameters.setFlashMode(mParameters.FLASH_MODE_OFF);
    mCamera.setParameters(mParameters);
    mCamera.stopPreview();
    isFlashLightOn = false;
}

public void onSensorChanged(SensorEvent event) {
    distanceFromPhone = event.values[0];
```

```
if(distanceFromPhone < mSensor.getMaximumRange()) {
    if(!isFlashLightOn) {
        turnTorchLightOn();
    }
} else {
    if(isFlashLightOn) {
        turnTorchLightOff();
    }
}
}
```

What just happened?

We used the standard steps for getting values from the proximity sensor and then used these values to turn on and off the camera flashlight in the phone. If any object comes within the range of the proximity sensor, it will turn on the flashlight; when the object goes away from its range, it will turn off the flashlight. You can determine a sensor's maximum range by using the getMaximumRange() method on the proximity sensor object.

Time for action – adjusting the screen brightness using the light sensor

One of the most common use cases for the light sensor is to adjust the screen brightness according to the external lighting conditions. The maximum range of the light sensor might be different on different Android devices, but most of them support from 0 lux to several thousand lux. Lux is the standard unit for measuring the luminance of the light falling on a surface. For our example, we will use a range from 0 to 100 lux, as normal indoor lighting falls within this range. But for sunlight and strong lights the range can go up to 1,000 lux or more. In the sample app, we will increase the screen brightness, when the indoor lighting goes low, and similarly we will decrease the screen brightness when it goes high.

1. We followed the standard steps to get values from the sensor. We select the sensor type to the TYPE_LIGHT in the getDefaultSensor() method of SensorManager. We also called the custom initScreenBrightness() method from onCreate() to initialize the required content resolver and current window objects:

   ```
   public class LightSensorActivity extends Activity implements
   SensorEventListener{
   ```

```
private SensorManager mSensorManager;
private Sensor mSensor;
private boolean isSensorPresent;
private ContentResolver mContentResolver;
private Window mWindow;

@Override
protected void onCreate(Bundle savedInstanceState) {
  super.onCreate(savedInstanceState);
  setContentView(R.layout.lightsensor_layout);

  mSensorManager = (SensorManager)this.getSystemService
  (Context.SENSOR_SERVICE);
  if(mSensorManager.getDefaultSensor(Sensor.TYPE_LIGHT) != null)
  {
    mSensor = mSensorManager.getDefaultSensor(Sensor.TYPE_LIGHT);
    isSensorPresent = true;
  } else {
    isSensorPresent = false;
  }
  initScreenBrightness();
}
```

2. As a standard practice, we registered the listener in the `onResume()` method and un-registered it in the `onPause()` method. Inside the custom `initScreenBrightness()` method, we initialized the `ContentResolver` and `Window` objects. The `ContentResolver` provides a handle to the system settings and the `Window` object provides the access to the current visible window. In the `onDestroy()` method of the activity, we change all the initialized objects references to null:

```
@Override
protected void onResume() {
  super.onResume();
  if(isSensorPresent) {
    mSensorManager.registerListener(this, mSensor,
    SensorManager.SENSOR_DELAY_NORMAL);
  }
}

@Override
protected void onPause() {
  super.onPause();
  if(isSensorPresent) {
    mSensorManager.unregisterListener(this);
  }
}
```

```
public void initScreenBrightness()
{
  mContentResolver = getContentResolver();
  mWindow = getWindow();
}

@Override
protected void onDestroy() {
  super.onDestroy();

  mSensorManager = null;
  mSensor = null;
  mContentResolver = null;
  mWindow = null;
}
```

3. As discussed earlier, we will use a light range from 0 to 100 lux for our example. We will be adjusting the brightness for two objects: one for the current visible window (for which the brightness value lies between 0 and 1), and the second for the system preference (for which the brightness value lies between 0 and 255). In order to use the common brightness value for both the objects, we will stick to a value between 0 and 1, and for system brightness we will scale up by multiplying it by 255. Since we have to increase the screen brightness, as the outside lightening goes low and vice versa, we take the inverse of the light sensor values. Also to keep the range of the brightness value between 0 and 1, we use only light values between 0 and 100. We pass on the inverse of light values obtained from the light sensor in the `onSensorChanged()` method, as an argument to our custom `changeScreenBrightness()` method to update the current window and system screen brightness:

```
public void changeScreenBrightness(float brightness)
{
  //system setting brightness values ranges between 0-255
  //We scale up by multiplying by 255
  //This change brightness for over all system settings
  System.putInt(mContentResolver, System.SCREEN_BRIGHTNESS, (int)
  (brightness*255));
  //screen brightness values ranges between 0 - 1
  //This only changes brightness for the current window
  LayoutParams mLayoutParams = mWindow.getAttributes();
  mLayoutParams.screenBrightness = brightness;
  mWindow.setAttributes(mLayoutParams);
}

@Override
public void onSensorChanged(SensorEvent event) {
```

```
                   float light = event.values[0];
                   //We only use light sensor value between 0 - 100
                   //Before sending, we take the inverse of the value
                   //So that they remain in range of 0 - 1
                   if(light>0 && light<100) {
                     changeScreenBrightness(1/light);
                   }
               }
```

The app needs to have following three permissions to run the previous two examples:

- `<uses-permission android:name="android.permission.CAMERA" />`
- `<uses-permission android:name="android.permission.FLASHLIGHT" />`
- `<uses-permission android:name="android.permission.WRITE_SETTINGS" />`

The camera permission is required to access the camera object, flashlight permission is required to turn on and turn off the flashlight, and the write settings permission is required to change any system settings.

What just happened?

We used light luminance values in lux (coming from the light sensor) to adjust the screen brightness. When it is very dark (almost no light), then the light sensor provides very low sensor values. When we send this low light sensor value (the minimum possible value being 1) to the `changeScreenBrightness()` method, then it makes the screen the brightest by taking the inverse (which is again 1) of the light sensor value and scaling up by multiplying it by 255 (1 * 255 = 255 brightness value). Similarly, under good lighting conditions, when we send a high sensor value (the maximum possible value being 99 in our case), then it makes the screen as dim as possible by taking the inverse (1/99=0.01) of the light sensor value and scaling up by multiplying it by 255 (0.01 * 255 = 2.55 brightness value). One of the easiest ways to test this app is to cover the light sensor with your hand or any opaque object. By doing this, you will observe that when you cover the light sensor, the screen becomes bright, and when you remove the cover, it becomes dim.

Wake locks, wakeup sensors, and the FIFO queue

All Android applications run on a dedicated **Application Processor** (**AP**), which is a part of the main CPU of the phone. This application processor is designed in such a way that it goes into the suspended mode when the user is not interacting with the phone. In this suspended mode, it reduces the power consumption by 10 times or more, but this freezes all the applications in the background. To work around this problem, the Android platform provides a solution using wake locks. If an application has to perform some important operation in the background and doesn't want the application processor to go into suspended mode, then it has to request a wake lock from the system's power service. Once the important operation is completed, it should release the wake lock. Wake lock can be obtained using the `PowerManager` object, which is provided by the system power service. The `newWakeLock()` method of `PowerManager` provides the object of wake lock. This `newWakeLock()` method accepts the type of wake lock and string tag for identification purposes. Once the wake lock object is instantiated, we need to call the `acquire()` method of the wake lock object to make it active and the `release()` method to make it inactive. The following code snippet shows how to acquire and release a wake lock:

```
PowerManager pm = (PowerManager)getSystemService(Context.POWER_SERVICE);
mWakeLock = pm.newWakeLock(PowerManager.PARTIAL_WAKE_LOCK, "myLock");
mWakeLock.acquire();
 //Do some important work in background.
 mWakeLock.release();
```

Wakeup and non-wakeup sensors

Android categorizes sensors into two types: wakeup and non-wakeup sensors. If the application processor has gone into suspended mode, then the wake up sensor will wake up the application processor from its suspended mode to report the sensor events to the application. The wakeup sensors ensure that their data is delivered independently of the state of the AP and before the maximum reporting latency has elapsed. Non-wakeup sensors do not wake up the AP out of its suspended mode to report data. If the AP is in suspended mode, the sensor events for the non-wakeup sensors are still collected in their hardware FIFO queue, but they are not delivered to the application. From the API level 21 (Lollipop) onward, Android platforms support the `isWakeUpSensor()` method to check the type of sensor.

The sensor's hardware FIFO queue

Non-wakeup sensors might have their own hardware FIFO queue. This FIFO (First In First Out) queue is used to store the sensor events while the AP is in suspended mode. These sensor events stored in the FIFO queue are delivered to the application when the AP wakes up. If the FIFO queue is too small to store all the events generated, then the older events are dropped to accommodate the newer ones. Some sensors might not have this FIFO queue at all. We can easily check the existence and size of the FIFO queue by using the `maxFifoEventCount()` method on the sensor object. If the value from this method comes to zero, it means that the FIFO count for that sensor doesn't exit.

If your application is using non-wakeup sensors in the background and performing a critical operation, and you don't want the AP to go into suspended mode, then you should use wake lock. But make sure you release the wake lock after the critical operation is done. Wake lock doesn't allow the application processor to go into suspended mode, but it also increases the power consumption. So, we have to make sure we release the wake lock after the critical operation is done; otherwise it will keep on draining the battery.

Summary

In this chapter, we looked at the two new proximity and light sensors and developed a small app using them. We also learned how to turn on and turn off the flashlight using the proximity sensor and adjust the screen brightness using the light sensor. We understood how to wake up the application processor when it's in suspended mode using wake locks. We looked at the wakeup and non-wake up sensors and their FIFO queues.

In the next chapter, we will learn about motion sensors (accelerometer, gyroscope, linear acceleration, gravity, and significant motion) and position sensors (magnetometer and orientation). We will also explore the newly introduced fingerprint sensor.

5
The Motion, Position, and Fingerprint Sensors

This chapter will introduce you to the motion, position, and fingerprint sensors. We will learn in detail about all the motion sensors (accelerometer, gyroscope, linear acceleration, gravity, and significant motion) and position sensors (magnetometer and orientation). As a learning exercise for the chapter, we will develop three small applications. The first application will detect a shake using the accelerometer sensor, the second one will tell the earth's magnetic field direction using the orientation sensor, and the third one will use the fingerprint sensor to authenticate the user.

The topics covered in this chapter are as follows:

- Understanding the motion-based sensors (accelerometer, gyroscope, linear acceleration, gravity, and significant motion sensors)
- Understanding the position-based sensors (magnetometer and orientation sensors)
- Understanding the newly introduced fingerprint sensor and its supporting APIs
- How to use the accelerometer sensor to detect the shaking of a phone
- How to use the orientation sensor and alternative API to build a compass
- How to use the fingerprint sensor to authenticate the user

Understanding motion-based sensors

Motion sensors are responsible for measuring acceleration forces and rotational forces acting along three axes of the phone. Motion sensors include the accelerometer, the gyroscope, gravity, linear acceleration, signification motion, the step detector, and the step counter. The detailed list of motion sensors can be found in `Chapter 1`, *Sensor Fundamentals*. In the next section, we will be discussing these sensors individually in detail. We will cover the step detector and step counter in the next chapter.

The accelerometer sensor

The accelerometer sensor determines the acceleration along the x, y, and z axes, which is applied to a phone by measuring the forces acting on the phone. The measured acceleration includes both the physical acceleration (change of velocity) and the static gravity acting on the phone all the time. Accelerometer sensors are made up of the **Micro Electro Mechanical System (MEMS)**, which is an embedded system that integrates electronic and mechanical components on a very small scale. The general principle of working of the smart phone accelerometer is based on the displacement of microscopic crystal plates, also called **seismic mass**, in the x, y, and z directions over the microscopic crystal base structure, as shown in the following diagram. When the phone is moved because of any user-generated force, the seismic mass also moves relative to the base structure located in between the plates of seismic mass, which produces a change in capacitance. This change in capacitance is converted to force using electric circuits. Additional algorithms are applied to calibrate the accelerometer values to compensate for the temperature, bias, and scale. The value reported by the accelerometer sensor is in SI units (m/s^2). When the phone is kept still without any motion, then the accelerometer sensor shows $9.81 m/s^2$ of gravitational force acting on the phone, and when the phone is in free fall, it shows zero force acting on the phone.

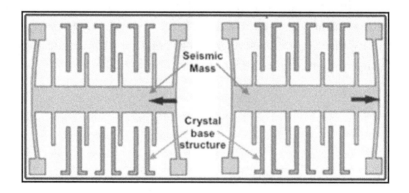

The gyroscope sensor

The gyroscope sensor reports the rate of rotation of the device around the x, y, and z axes. The gyroscope sensor works by sensing the change in capacitance between two microscopic crystal structures due to the effect of rotational forces acting on them. The general principle of working of the smart phone gyroscope is based on displacement of the microscopic crystal circular plate also called the proof mass in the x, y and z directions, over the underlying microscopic crystal base or plate, as shown in the following diagram. When the user rotates the phone, the proof mass (center plate) moves over the capacitor plates located underneath the proof mass, which produces a change in capacitance. This change in capacitance is converted to a rate of rotation using electric circuits. Additional algorithms are applied to calibrate the gyroscope values to compensate for the temperature, drift, and scale. There are two types of values given by the gyroscope sensor: calibrated and uncalibrated. The uncalibrated values are the raw values without the drift compensation and can be requested from SensorManager by specifying the TYPE_GYROSCOPE_UNCALIBRATED constant, while the calibrated values can be obtained by requesting the TYPE_GYROSCOPE constant. For most use cases, we should use the calibrated gyroscope values, and it is only if we are applying our own calibration algorithms that we should use un-calibrated values. The values are reported in units of radians per second (rad/s).

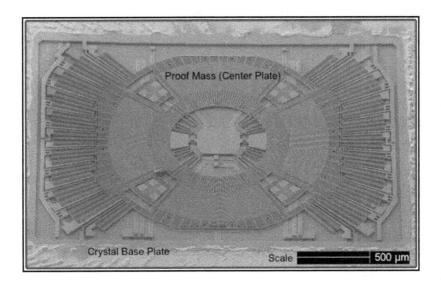

The gravity sensor

The gravity sensor is a software sensor and it reports the force of gravity acting along the x, y, and z axes. It uses the same accelerometer sensor unit (m/s^2) to report values. The gravity values are computed by removing the user-generated forces acting on the phone. It uses the accelerometer as its underlying hardware sensor.

The linear acceleration sensor

The linear acceleration sensor is a software sensor and is responsible for reporting the acceleration force acting on the x, y, and z axes of the phone after excluding the gravity force. It also uses the same unit (m/s^2) to report values that is used by the gravity and accelerometer sensors. Linear acceleration values are calculated by removing the force of gravity acting on each axis of the phone. It uses the accelerometer as its underlying hardware sensor. Conceptually, the accelerometer sensor values are a summation of the linear acceleration and gravity:

Accelerometer value = Linear Acceleration value + Gravity value.

The significant motion sensor

The signification motion sensor is a software sensor, and it uses the accelerometer as its underlying hardware sensor. It triggers an event every time a signification motion on the phone takes place. Walking, biking, or sitting in a moving car are examples of signification motions. It has a one-shot reporting mode and hence will be disabled automatically once it is triggered. Further details on reporting modes can be found in Chapter 1, *Sensor Fundamentals*. We need to request the significant motion as many times as we want to trigger it. The way to set up the significant motion sensor is slightly different than other sensors, which are done using SensorManager. The significant motion event trigger callback is set using the object of TriggerEventListener. The following is the code snippet to set up, request, and cancel the signification motion sensor:

```
public class SigMotionActivity extends Activity{

    private SensorManager mSensorManager;
    private Sensor mSensor;
    private TriggerEventListener mTriggerEventListener;

    @Override
    protected void onCreate(Bundle savedInstanceState) {
        super.onCreate(savedInstanceState);
```

```
    mSensorManager = (SensorManager)
    getSystemService(Context.SENSOR_SERVICE);
    mSensor = mSensorManager.getDefaultSensor
    (Sensor.TYPE_SIGNIFICANT_MOTION);

    mTriggerEventListener = new TriggerEventListener() {
        @Override
        public void onTrigger(TriggerEvent event) {
            // Take action
        }
    };
}

@Override
protected void onResume() {
    super.onResume();
    mSensorManager.requestTriggerSensor
    (mTriggerEventListener, mSensor);
}

@Override
protected void onPause() {
    super.onPause();
    mSensorManager.cancelTriggerSensor(mTriggerEventListener, mSensor);
}
}
```

Understanding position-based sensors

The position sensor lets your app determine the position of a device. There are two major sensors in this category: the geomagnetic field sensor and the orientation sensor. The proximity sensor, which measures the proximity of any object to the phone, also comes under this category. The proximity sensor has already been discussed in the previous chapter in detail.

The magnetometer sensor

The magnetometer sensor measures the changes in the earth's magnetic field. It provides the raw magnetic field strength in units of micro tesla (μT). The magnetometer sensor is based on a miniature Hall effect sensor, which detects the earth's magnetic field along the three perpendicular *x*, *y*, and *z* axes. The Hall effect sensor measures the magnetic field by generating a voltage that is proportional to the earth's magnetic field strength and polarity. This voltage is converted to micro tesla (μT) values using electric circuits. The magnetometer sensor provides two types of value: calibrated and uncalibrated. The uncalibrated values are the raw values without the hard iron calibration applied to them, and they can be requested from `SensorManager` by specifying the `TYPE_MAGNETIC_FIELD_UNCALIBRATED` constant, while the calibrated values can be obtained by requesting the `TYPE_MAGNETIC_FIELD` constant. Factory calibration and temperature compensation are applied to both calibrated and uncalibrated values.

The orientation sensor

The orientation sensor is a software sensor and measures the position of the device relative to the earth's frame of reference. The orientation sensor drives its data by processing the raw values of the accelerometer and magnetometer sensors. It provides the position by giving the azimuth, pitch, and roll angles. One of the most common use cases of the orientation sensor is to build a magnetic compass on the phone.

- Azimuth is defined as the degree of rotation made by the phone around the z axis. It can be also seen as the angle between the magnetic north and the phone's *y* axis. When the phone's *y* axis is aligned with the earth's magnetic north direction, then its value is zero degrees. The Azimuth value can vary from 0 to 360 degrees. We will use the azimuth value to create our compass in the next section.
- Pitch is defined as the degree of rotation made by the phone around the *x* axis. Its value can vary from 180 to -180 degrees. When the phone's positive *z* axis rotates towards the positive *y* axis, then pitch's value is positive, but if the phone's positive *z* axis rotates towards the negative *y* axis, then pitch's value is negative.
- Roll is defined as the degree of rotation made by the phone around the *y* axis. Its value can vary from 90 to -90 degrees. When the phone's positive *z* axis rotates towards the positive *x* axis, then roll's value is positive, but if the phone's positive *z* axis rotates towards the negative *x* axis, then roll's value is negative.

Note that since Android 2.2 (API Level 8), the orientation sensor has been deprecated. The reason for deprecation was accuracy and precision issues, as this sensor is only reliable when the roll component is 0. Also, this sensor involves heavy processing from the accelerometer and magnetometer sensors. Instead of using raw values from the orientation sensor, it is recommended that you use the `getRotationMatrix()` method in conjunction with the `getOrientation()` method of `SensorManager` to compute the same orientation values that are given by the orientation sensor. We will see more details on this in the next section when we develop our compass using both the orientation sensor and alternative APIs.

The fingerprint sensor

Samsung was the first to introduce the fingerprint sensor in their Android devices, and they also provided support for it in their Pass SDK. The official support for fingerprint sensors was provided in the Android platform from Android 6.0 (API Level 23). The fingerprint sensor is a hardware sensor; generally it is found either at the back of the Android phone, or at the bottom of the screen. Typically, two types of fingerprint sensor are found today: the first one is a capacitive sensor, and the second one is an optical sensor. An optical sensor works by shining a bright light over your fingerprint and taking a digital photograph. This digital image is compared with the original fingerprint digital image to get the authentication results. The capacitive sensor is found in most iPhones and Android phones today. It works by passing a mild electric current through the outer skin of your finger. When your finger is placed on the surface of the sensor, the ridges in your fingerprints touch the surface while the hollows between the ridges stand clear of it. The capacitive sensor captures these varying distances between ridges and hollow places and builds a digital image of the fingerprint. This digital image is then verified with the original fingerprint. We will look at the fingerprint APIs and implementation details in the next section.

Time for action – shake detection using the accelerometer sensor

One of the most common use cases of the accelerometer sensor is to detect the shaking of the phone. Shaking can act as a valuable input for the apps, especially when the phone screen is off. For example, a lot of music player apps allow you to change the songs just by shaking the phone. In our example, we will play a small audio MP3 file when the phone shake is detected using the accelerometer sensor:

1. As the first step, we create the necessary infrastructure to get the values from the accelerometer sensor. We will create a ShakeDetectionActivity and follow the standard steps for getting values from a sensor. We will select the sensor type for TYPE_ACCELEROMETER in the getDefaultSensor() method of SensorManager and initiate the MediaPlayer object with the audio MP3 file kept in the raw folder inside the onCreate() method of the activity. As a standard practice, we will register the listener in onResume() and un-register it in the onPause() methods:

```
public class ShakeDetectionActivity extends Activity implements
SensorEventListener {

    private SensorManager mSensorManager;
    private Sensor mAccelerometer;
    private float x,y,z,last_x,last_y,last_z;
    private boolean isFirstValue;
    private float shakeThreshold = 3f;
    private MediaPlayer mMediaPlayer;

    @Override
    protected void onCreate(Bundle savedInstanceState) {
        super.onCreate(savedInstanceState);
        setContentView(R.layout.shakedetection_layout);
        mSensorManager = (SensorManager)getSystemService
        (SENSOR_SERVICE);
        mAccelerometer = mSensorManager.getDefaultSensor
        (Sensor.TYPE_ACCELEROMETER);
        mMediaPlayer = MediaPlayer.create(getApplicationContext(),
        R.raw.mario);
    }

    protected void onResume() {
        super.onResume();
        mSensorManager.registerListener(this, mAccelerometer,
        SensorManager.SENSOR_DELAY_UI);
```

```
    }

  protected void onPause() {
    super.onPause();
    mSensorManager.unregisterListener(this, mAccelerometer);
  }
}
```

2. Inside the `onSensorChanged()` method, we write our core logic to detect shakes. When we shake the phone with our hands, the accelerometer sensor measures the force acting on the phone. There is a huge variation in the force acting on the phone during the shake. We measure this variation or change in the acceleration. If the change in acceleration in any two axes crosses a threshold of 3 m/s^2, then we consider it a shake. The threshold of 3 m/s^2 can only be reached by shaking the phone with the hands. To calculate the change in acceleration, we take the absolute difference between the current and last known accelerometer values, and if the absolute difference is greaten than 3m/s^2 in any two axes, then we play the sound:

```
@Override
public void onSensorChanged(SensorEvent event) {

  x = event.values[0];
  y = event.values[1];
  z = event.values[2];
  if(isFirstValue) {
    float deltaX = Math.abs(last_x - x);
    float deltaY = Math.abs(last_y - y);
    float deltaZ = Math.abs(last_z - z);
    // If the values of acceleration have changed on at least two
    axes, then we assume that we are in a shake motion
    if((deltaX > shakeThreshold && deltaY > shakeThreshold)
    || (deltaX > shakeThreshold && deltaZ > shakeThreshold)
    || (deltaY > shakeThreshold && deltaZ > shakeThreshold)) {
      //Don't play sound, if it is already being played
      if(!mMediaPlayer.isPlaying()) {
        //Play the sound, when Phone is Shaking
        mMediaPlayer.start();
      }
    }
  }
  last_x = x;
  last_y = y;
  last_z = z;
  isFirstValue = true;
}
```

Time for action – the compass using orientation sensor and orientation APIs

In our example, we will use the orientation sensor to develop the compass, and since it is a deprecated sensor, we will also develop it using alternative APIs. From the orientation sensor, we will directly use its azimuth values to feed into the compass, while for alternative APIs, we will use the raw accelerometer and magnetometer sensor values to compute the azimuth values. Let's look at both the implementations in detail:

1. First, we create the infrastructure to get the values from the orientation, accelerometer, and magnetometer sensors. Inside the onCreate() method of CompassActivity, we initialize all the three sensors using SensorManager. We also initiate a layout file for the activity, which consists of a compass image that has North, South, East, and West marked on it. The compass image will be rotated to align its north to point toward the Earth's magnetic north. We also created four float arrays to store the sensor's value in it. As a standard practice, we registered the listener in onResume() and un-registered it in the onPause() method:

```
public class CompassActivity extends Activity implements
SensorEventListener {

  private ImageView mCompass;
  private SensorManager mSensorManager;
  private Sensor mAccelerometerSensor, mMagnetometerSensor,
  mOrientationSensor;
  private float[] mLastAccelerometer = new float[3];
  private float[] mLastMagnetometer = new float[3];
  private float[] mRotationMatrix = new float[9];
  private float[] mOrientation = new float[3];
  private boolean mLastAccelerometerSet = false;
  private boolean mLastMagnetometerSet = false;
  private float mCurrentDegree = 0f;
  private boolean useOrientationAPI = false;
  private long lastUpdateTime = 0;

  @Override
  protected void onCreate(Bundle savedInstanceState) {
    super.onCreate(savedInstanceState);
    setContentView(R.layout.compass_layout);
    mSensorManager = (SensorManager)getSystemService
    (SENSOR_SERVICE);
    mAccelerometerSensor = mSensorManager.getDefaultSensor
    (Sensor.TYPE_ACCELEROMETER);
```

```
    mMagnetometerSensor = mSensorManager.getDefaultSensor
    (Sensor.TYPE_MAGNETIC_FIELD);
    mOrientationSensor = mSensorManager.getDefaultSensor
    (Sensor.TYPE_ORIENTATION);
    mCompass = (ImageView)
    findViewById(R.id.compass);
}

protected void onResume() {
    super.onResume();
    if(useOrientationAPI) {
        mSensorManager.registerListener(this, mAccelerometerSensor,
        SensorManager.SENSOR_DELAY_UI);
        mSensorManager.registerListener(this, mMagnetometerSensor,
        SensorManager.SENSOR_DELAY_UI);
    } else{
        mSensorManager.registerListener(this, mOrientationSensor,
        SensorManager.SENSOR_DELAY_UI);
    }
}

protected void onPause() {
    super.onPause();
    if(useOrientationAPI) {
        mSensorManager.unregisterListener
        (this, mAccelerometerSensor);
        mSensorManager.unregisterListener(this, mMagnetometerSensor);
    } else {
        mSensorManager.unregisterListener(this, mOrientationSensor);
    }
}
```

2. We used a `useOrientationAPI` Boolean variable to select the input source for the compass. If the `useOrientationAPI` Boolean variable is true, then we use input from the accelerometer and magnetometer sensors and feed it into the alternative APIs (`getRotationMatrix()` and `getOrientation()`) to get the Earth's magnetic north angle, while if it is false, then we use input from the orientation sensor to get the earth's magnetic north angle.

The `rotateUsingOrientationSensor()` method accepts the object of `SensorEvent` that contains the orientation sensor values and is responsible for rotating the compass image and keeping it aligned to the earth's magnetic north direction. It uses the `RotateAnimation` class to make the rotation animation of the compass image. The `RotateAnimation` class is an Android built in animation utility that can rotate any UI object on the *x* and *y* axes. The constructor accepts lot optional parameters, such as the starting angle of rotation, the end of angle of rotation, the center of rotation, and so on. The rotation animation is carried only four times in one second to make the rotation look smooth. The azimuth angle, which is the first value given by the orientation sensor, is used to align the direction of the compass image:

```
@Override
public void onSensorChanged(SensorEvent event) {
  if(useOrientationAPI) {
    rotateUsingOrientationAPI(event);
  } else {
    rotateUsingOrientationSensor(event);
  }
}

public void rotateUsingOrientationSensor(SensorEvent event){
  //only 4 times in 1 second
  if(System.currentTimeMillis() - lastUpdateTime > 250)    {
    float angleInDegress = event.values[0];
    RotateAnimation mRotateAnimation = new RotateAnimation(
    mCurrentDegree, -angleInDegress,
    Animation.RELATIVE_TO_SELF, 0.5f,
    Animation.RELATIVE_TO_SELF, 0.5f);
    //250 milliseconds
    mRotateAnimation.setDuration(250);
    mRotateAnimation.setFillAfter(true);
    mCompass.startAnimation(mRotateAnimation);
    mCurrentDegree = -angleInDegress;
    lastUpdateTime = System.currentTimeMillis();
  }
}
```

3. The `rotateUsingOrientationAPI()` method is used to rotate the compass using the `getRotationMatrix()` and `getOrientation()` APIs. This method assigns the accelerometer sensor values to the `mLastAccelerometer` float array and the magnetometer sensor values to the `mLastMagnetometer` float array. Once we have both the accelerometer and magnetometer sensor values, then they are passed into the `getRotationMatrix()` API to get the rotation matrix, which is further passed into the `getOrientation()` API to get the orientation values. These orientation values are converted from radians to degrees and then used to rotate the compass image, as done inside the `rotateUsingOrientationSensor()` method. It uses the same `RotateAnimation` class to make the rotation animation of the compass image, as discussed in the previous section:

```
public void rotateUsingOrientationAPI(SensorEvent event){
    if (event.sensor == mAccelerometerSensor) {
        System.arraycopy(event.values, 0, mLastAccelerometer, 0,
        event.values.length);
        mLastAccelerometerSet = true;
    } else if (event.sensor == mMagnetometerSensor) {
        System.arraycopy(event.values, 0, mLastMagnetometer, 0,
        event.values.length);
        mLastMagnetometerSet = true;
    }//only 4 times in 1 second
    if (mLastAccelerometerSet && mLastMagnetometerSet &&
    System.currentTimeMillis() - lastUpdateTime > 250)
    {
        SensorManager.getRotationMatrix(mRotationMatrix, null,
        mLastAccelerometer, mLastMagnetometer);
        SensorManager.getOrientation(mRotationMatrix, mOrientation);
        float azimuthInRadians = mOrientation[0];
        float azimuthInDegress = (float)
        (Math.toDegrees(azimuthInRadians)+360)%360;
        RotateAnimation mRotateAnimation = new RotateAnimation(
        mCurrentDegree, -azimuthInDegress,
        Animation.RELATIVE_TO_SELF, 0.5f,
        Animation.RELATIVE_TO_SELF, 0.5f);
        mRotateAnimation.setDuration(250);
        mRotateAnimation.setFillAfter(true);
        mCompass.startAnimation(mRotateAnimation);
        mCurrentDegree = -azimuthInDegress;
        lastUpdateTime = System.currentTimeMillis();
    }
}
```

The following is a screenshot of the compass on a Nexus 5P device:

Time for action – using the fingerprint sensor

In order to support the fingerprint sensor, the Android platform has introduced a new system service, which is called the Finger Print Service, and it can be accessed using the instance of `FingerprintManager`. It provides all the necessary APIs to use the fingerprint sensor. In the following example, we will use the fingerprint sensor to authenticate the user. In order to make this example work, the Android device should have a fingerprint sensor, and it also should have set up or enrolled the user's fingerprint using the security settings. We also need to use two components of security (Keystore and Cipher) to use the fingerprint authentication API. Fingerprint sensor APIs require install time permission in the `AndroidManifest.xml` file (`android.permission.USE_FINGERPRINT`) and also runtime permission before using them. Now, let's look at the implementation details:

1. Inside the `onCreate()` method of `FingerPrintActivity`, we initiated the object of `FingerprintManager` using `getSystemService(FINGERPRINT_SERVICE)`.
   The `checkFingerPrintConditions()` method is responsible for checking the necessary conditions for the Fingerprint sensor to work. This method is invoked from `onCreate()` and also from the `initiateFingerPrintSensor()` method. We will discuss the `checkFingerPrintConditions()` method in the next section:

   ```
   public class FingerPrintActivity extends Activity {

       private static final int FINGERPRINT_PERMISSION_REQUEST_CODE = 0;
       private FingerprintManager mFingerprintManager;
       //Alias for our key in the Android Key Store
       private static final String KEY_NAME = "my_key";
       private KeyStore mKeyStore;
       private KeyGenerator mKeyGenerator;
       private Cipher mCipher;
       private CancellationSignal mCancellationSignal;
       private Dialog mFingerPrintDialog;

       @Override
       protected void onCreate(Bundle savedInstanceState) {
         super.onCreate(savedInstanceState);
         setContentView(R.layout.fingerprint_layout);
         mFingerprintManager = (FingerprintManager)getSystemService
         (FINGERPRINT_SERVICE);
         //As soon as Activity starts, check for the finger print
         conditions
   ```

```
        checkFingerPrintConditions()
    }

    public void initiateFingerPrintSensor(View v) {
        //Called from Layout button
        checkFingerPrintConditions();
    }
```

2. There are three mandatory conditions for the fingerprint sensor to work; they are checked inside the `checkFingerPrintConditions()` method. The first condition is to check if the fingerprint sensor hardware is present on the phone, which is done by the `isHardwareDetected()` method of `FingerprintManager`. The second condition is to check whether the user has enrolled or set up his fingerprint; this is done by using the `hasEnrolledFingerprints()` method. The third and final condition is to check whether the user has given runtime permission to use the fingerprint sensor. This is done using the `checkSelfPermission()` method of the `ContextCompat` class. If the user has not given the runtime permission, then we ask for it using the `requestPermissions()` method. This will open a runtime permission dialog, and when the user allows it, we will receive a callback in the `onRequestPermissionsResult()` method. Once all the conditions are satisfied and we have the required permission, we invoke the `showFingerPrintDialog()` method, which will initiate the fingerprint authentication process explained in the next section. If any of the conditions fail, we show the relevant message using the `showAlertDialog()` method. This method simply presents the user with the passed title and message:

```
    public void checkFingerPrintConditions() {

        if(mFingerprintManager.isHardwareDetected()) {
            if(mFingerprintManager.hasEnrolledFingerprints()) {
                if(ContextCompat.checkSelfPermission(this,
                Manifest.permission.USE_FINGERPRINT) !=
                PackageManager.PERMISSION_GRANTED) {
                    //Requesting runtime finger print permission
                    requestPermissions(new String[]
                    {Manifest.permission.USE_FINGERPRINT},
                    FINGERPRINT_PERMISSION_REQUEST_CODE);
                } else {
                    //After all 3 conditions are met, then show FingerPrint
                    Dialog
                    showFingerPrintDialog();
                }
            } else {
                showAlertDialog("Finger Print Not Registered!", "Go to
```

```
        'Settings -> Security -> Fingerprint' and register at least
        one fingerprint");
      }
    } else {
      showAlertDialog("Finger Print Sensor Not Found!", "Finger Print
      Sensor could not be found on your phone.");
    }
  }

  @Override
  public void onRequestPermissionsResult(int requestCode, String[]
  permissions, int[] state) {

    //show FingerPrint Dialog, when runtime permission is granted
    if (requestCode == FINGERPRINT_PERMISSION_REQUEST_CODE
    && state[0] == PackageManager.PERMISSION_GRANTED) {

      showFingerPrintDialog();
    }
  }

  public void showAlertDialog(String title, String message){
    new android.app.AlertDialog.Builder(this).setTitle(title)
    .setMessage(message).setIcon(android.R.drawable.ic_dialog_alert)
    .setPositiveButton("Cancel", new DialogInterface
    .OnClickListener()
    {
        public void onClick(DialogInterface dialog, int whichButton)
        {
          dialog.dismiss();
        }})
      .show();
  }
```

3. The `showFingerPrintDialog()` method performs two major tasks: the first task is to initiate the required fingerprint APIs and settings, which is done by calling the `initFingerPrintSettings()` method, and the second task is to show a custom dialog, which asks the user to place their finger on the fingerprint sensor for authentication. If any of the required APIs or settings fail, then we show the relevant error message to the user. The `initFingerPrintSettings()` method initiates the `Keystore`, `Cipher`, and object of the `CancellationSignal` class. We will discuss `Keystore` and `Cipher` in the next section.

The cancel() method of the CancellationSignal class instructs the authentication API to stop sensing for the fingerprint. Once all three (Keystore,Cipher, and CancellationSignal) are initiated successfully, we invoke the authenticate() method of FingerprintManager. This wakes up the fingerprint sensor hardware, and it starts sensing for a fingerprint. This is the time that the user has to place his finger on the fingerprint sensor for authentication. Generally, the fingerprint sensor declares the authentication result within a second. The result callback of fingerprint authentication is done through the object of the FingerprintManager.AuthenticationCallback class, which is discussed in the last section of this example:

```
public void showFingerPrintDialog() {
  //First Initialize the FingerPrint Settings
  if(initFingerPrintSettings())
  {
    //Init Custom FingerPrint Dialog from xml
    mFingerPrintDialog = new Dialog(this);
    View view = LayoutInflater.from(this).inflate
    (R.layout.fingerpring_dialog, null, false);
    mFingerPrintDialog.setContentView(view);
    Button cancel = (Button) view.findViewById(R.id.cancelbutton);
    cancel.setOnClickListener(new View.OnClickListener() {
      @Override
      public void onClick(View arg0) {
        mCancellationSignal.cancel();
        mFingerPrintDialog.dismiss();
      }
    });

    //Stops the cancelling of the fingerprint dialog
    //by back press or touching accidentally on screen
    mFingerPrintDialog.setCanceledOnTouchOutside(false);
    mFingerPrintDialog.setCancelable(false);
    mFingerPrintDialog.show();
  }
  else
  {
    showAlertDialog("Error!", "Error in initiating Finger Print
    Cipher or Key!");
  }
}

public boolean initFingerPrintSettings() {

  //CancellationSignal requests authenticate api to stop scanning
  mCancellationSignal = new CancellationSignal();
```

```
      if(initKey() && initCipher()) {
        mFingerprintManager.authenticate(new
        FingerprintManager.CryptoObject(mCipher),
        mCancellationSignal, 0, new AuthenticationListener(), null);
        return true;
      } else {
        return false;
      }
    }
```

4. Inside the `initCipher()` method, we initialize the `Cipher` instance with the created key in the `initkey()` method. It returns true if the initialization was successful and returns false if the lock screen is disabled or reset after the key was generated, or if a fingerprint got enrolled after the key was generated.
   The `initkey()` method creates a symmetric key in the Android key store, which can only be used after the user has been authenticated by a fingerprint. The detailed discussion of `Cipher` and `Keystore` belongs to security and is out of the scope of this book:

```
    public boolean initKey() {
      try {
        mKeyStore = KeyStore.getInstance("AndroidKeyStore");
        mKeyStore.load(null);
        mKeyGenerator = KeyGenerator.getInstance
        (KeyProperties.KEY_ALGORITHM_AES, "AndroidKeyStore");
        mKeyGenerator.init(new KeyGenParameterSpec.Builder(KEY_NAME,
        KeyProperties.PURPOSE_ENCRYPT | KeyProperties.PURPOSE_DECRYPT)
        .setBlockModes(KeyProperties.BLOCK_MODE_CBC)
        .setUserAuthenticationRequired(true)
        .setEncryptionPaddings(KeyProperties.ENCRYPTION_PADDING_PKCS7)
        .build());
        mKeyGenerator.generateKey();
        return true;
      } catch (Exception e) {
        return false;
      }
    }

    public boolean initCipher() {
      try {
        mKeyStore.load(null);
        SecretKey key = (SecretKey) mKeyStore.getKey(KEY_NAME, null);
        mCipher = Cipher.getInstance(KeyProperties.KEY_ALGORITHM_AES +
        "/" + KeyProperties.BLOCK_MODE_CBC + "/" +
        KeyProperties.ENCRYPTION_PADDING_PKCS7);
        mCipher.init(Cipher.ENCRYPT_MODE, key);
        return true;
```

```
    } catch (KeyStoreException | CertificateException |
    UnrecoverableKeyException | IOException |
    NoSuchAlgorithmException | InvalidKeyException |
    NoSuchPaddingException e) {
      return false;
    }
  }
```

5. The `AuthenticationListener` class is responsible for passing the result callback from the `FingerprintManager` authentication API. Once the authentication is done, the relevant method is called depending on the result of authentication. If the authentication is successful, which means that the recognized fingerprint matches with the original enrolled fingerprint, then we show a success message to the user via the Toast API. In case of failure, which means that the recognized fingerprint doesn't match the originally enrolled fingerprint, we show the relevant failure message. In case of error, which means that there was an error in reading the fingerprint, we show the relevant error message:

```
class AuthenticationListener extends
FingerprintManager.AuthenticationCallback{

  @Override
  public void onAuthenticationError(int errMsgId, CharSequence
  errString) {

    Toast.makeText(getApplicationContext(), "Authentication
    Error!", Toast.LENGTH_LONG).show();
  }

  @Override
  public void onAuthenticationHelp(int helpMsgId, CharSequence
  helpString) {
  }

  @Override
  public void onAuthenticationFailed() {

    Toast.makeText(getApplicationContext(), "Authentication
    Failed!", Toast.LENGTH_LONG).show();
  }

  @Override
  public void onAuthenticationSucceeded
  (FingerprintManager.AuthenticationResult result) {
      Toast.makeText(getApplicationContext(), "Authentication
```

```
        Success!", Toast.LENGTH_LONG).show();
        mFingerPrintDialog.dismiss();
    }
}
```

What just happened?

We just created three small applications using three different sensors. The first one detects physical shakes using the accelerometer sensor, the second one tells the earth's magnetic direction using the orientation sensor, and the third one uses the fingerprint sensor to authenticate the user. A few important points to note are that the orientation sensor has been deprecated, so in place of it we should use the getRotationMatrix() and getOrientation() APIs to get the orientation values. Fingerprint APIs were introduced in Android Marshmallow (API Level 23), which uses both runtime and install time permissions. Thus, to use the fingerprint sensor, we should include both runtime and install time permissions.

Summary

We learned about all the motion sensors (accelerometer, gyroscope, linear acceleration, gravity, and significant motion) and position sensors (magnetometer and orientation) in detail. We also looked at the newly introduced fingerprint sensor and its supporting APIs.

In the next chapter, we will take our understanding of motion sensors (particularly the accelerometer) to the next level, and we will use the accelerometer sensor to develop an algorithm to detect walking, jogging, and running activities. We will also learn two new sensors, that is, the step detector and step counter.

6
The Step Counter and Detector Sensors – The Pedometer App

This chapter will focus on learning the use of the step detector and step counter sensors. We will analyze and process the accelerometer data to develop the algorithm for detecting the types of steps (walking, jogging, and fast running). As a learning exercise, we will develop a pedometer application and will closely look at the infrastructure (service, threads, and database) required to process the sensor data in the background for a longer duration of time. We will also discuss how to combine the step detector sensor with the accelerometer sensor to achieve battery optimization.

You will learn the following topics in this chapter:

- Understanding the requirements for the pedometer app using the step detector and accelerometer sensors
- Understanding the step detector and step counter sensors
- How to use the step counter sensor in activity and show the number of steps taken since the phone's last reboot
- How to use the step detector sensor in service and show the number of steps taken per day using the SQLite database
- Understanding the accelerometer sensor's behavior during walking, jogging, and fast running activities

- How to develop an algorithm to detect the types of steps (walking, jogging, and fast running) using the accelerometer sensor data and also achieve battery optimization using the sensor fusion between the step detector and accelerometer sensors
- How to derive the pedometer data matrix (total steps, distance, duration, average speed, average step frequency, calories burned, and type of steps) by using our steps detected algorithm

The pedometer app's requirements

We will be working on three incremental examples as learning assignments for this chapter. In the first example, we will be using the step counter sensor to show the number of steps taken since the phone was powered on in the activity. In our second example, we will go a little deeper and will discuss how to use the step detector sensor to store the steps information in the SQLite database from the service, and finally we will show the steps history along with the dates of using the activity. Our third example will be an evolved pedometer application that will use the sensor fusion between the step detector and accelerometer sensors to derive advanced functionality of the app. This evolved pedometer application will be highly battery optimized and will automatically track the physical activity (walking, jogging, and fast running) happening in the background. The following is a list of the high level requirements of this pedometer application:

1. Create a pedometer application that works in the background and tracks physical activity automatically
2. The pedometer application should be battery optimized and should go to sleep when there is no physical activity
3. The pedometer application should be able to differentiate between three physical activity types, that is, normal walking, jogging, or fast walking and fast running
4. The pedometer application should be able to log (in database), derive, and show (in the user interface) the following data matrix:

1. The total steps taken (per day)
2. The total distance travelled (per day)
3. The total duration (per day)
4. The average speed (per day)
5. The average step frequency (per day)
6. The calories burned (per day)
7. The type of physical activity (walking, jogging, or fast running)

Understanding the step counter and step detector sensors

The step counter and step detector sensors are very similar to each other and are used to count the steps. Both the sensors are based on a common hardware sensor that internally uses the accelerometer, but Android still treats them as logically separate sensors. Both of these sensors are highly battery optimized and consume very little power. Now, let's look at each individual sensor in detail.

The step counter sensor

The step counter sensor is used to get the total number of steps taken by the user since the last reboot (power on) of the phone. When the phone is restarted, the value of the step counter sensor is reset to zero. In the `onSensorChanged()` method, the number of steps is given by `event.value[0]`; although it's a float value, the fractional part is always zero. The event timestamp represents the time at which the last step was taken. This sensor is especially useful for those applications that don't want to run in the background and maintain the history of steps themselves. This sensor works in the batch and continuous modes. If we specify 0 or no latency in the `SensorManager.registerListener()` method, then it works in continuous mode, otherwise, if we specify any latency, then it groups the events in batches and reports them at a specified latency. For prolonged usage of this sensor, it's recommended that you use the batch mode, as it saves power. The step counter uses on change reporting mode, which means it reports the event as soon as there is a change in the value.

The step detector sensor

The step detector sensor triggers an event each time a step is taken by the user. The value reported in the `onSensorChanged()` method is always one, the fractional part is always zero, and the event timestamp is the moment that the user's foot hits the ground. The step detector sensor has very low latency in reporting the steps, which is generally within 1 and 2 seconds. The step detector sensor has lower accuracy and produces more false positives compared to the step counter sensor. The step counter sensor is more accurate, but it has more latency in reporting the steps, as it uses extra time after each step to remove any false positive values. The step detector sensor is recommended for those applications that want to track the steps in real time and maintain their own history of each and every step with their timestamp.

Time for action – using the step counter sensor in activity

In this section, we will learn how to use the step counter sensor with a simple example. The good thing about the step counter is that, unlike other sensors, your app doesn't need to tell the sensor when to start counting the steps and when to stop counting them. It automatically starts counting as soon as the phone is powered on. To use it, we just have to register the listener with the sensor manager and then unregister it after using it. In the following example, we will be showing the total number of steps taken by the user since the last reboot (power on) of the phone in the android activity:

1. We create a StepsCounterActivity, which implements the SensorEventListener interface so that it can receive the sensor events. We initiate the SensorManager and Sensor objects of the step counter, and we also check the sensor availability in the OnCreate() method of the activity. We register the listener in the onResume() method and unregistered it in the onPause() method as a standard practice. If we want the app to keep on counting the steps in the background, then ideally we should use Android service, and we should not unregister it. We use TextView to display the total number of steps taken and update the latest value in the onSensorChanged() method:

```
public class StepsCounterActivity extends Activity
implements SensorEventListener{

private SensorManager mSensorManager;
private Sensor mSensor;
private boolean isSensorPresent;
private TextView mStepsSinceReboot;

@Override
protected void onCreate(Bundle savedInstanceState){
  super.onCreate(savedInstanceState);
  setContentView(R.layout.stepcounter_layout);
  mStepsSinceReboot = (TextView)findViewById
  (R.id.stepssincereboot);
  mSensorManager = (SensorManager)
  this.getSystemService(Context.SENSOR_SERVICE);
  if(mSensorManager.getDefaultSensor
  (Sensor.TYPE_STEP_COUNTER) != null) {
    mSensor = mSensorManager.getDefaultSensor
    (Sensor.TYPE_STEP_COUNTER);
    isSensorPresent = true;
```

```
    } else {
      isSensorPresent = false;
    }
  }

  @Override
  protected void onResume() {
    super.onResume();
    if(isSensorPresent) {
      mSensorManager.registerListener(this, mSensor,
      SensorManager.SENSOR_DELAY_NORMAL);
    }
  }

  @Override
  protected void onPause() {
    super.onPause();
    if(isSensorPresent) {
      mSensorManager.unregisterListener(this);
    }
  }

  @Override
  public void onSensorChanged(SensorEvent event) {
    mStepsSinceReboot.setText("Steps since reboot:" +
    String.valueOf(event.values[0]));
  }
```

Time for action – maintaining step history with the step detector sensor

The step counter sensor works well when we have to deal with the total number of steps taken by the user since the last reboot (power on) of the phone. It doesn't cater to our purpose when we have to maintain the history of each and every step taken by the user. The step counter sensor may combine some steps and process them together and will only update with an aggregated count instead of reporting the individual step detail. For such cases, the step detector sensor is the right choice. In our example, we will be using the step detector sensor to store the details of each step taken by the user, and we will show the total number of steps for each day since the application was installed. Our example will consist of three major components of android, namely, service, the SQLite database, and activity.

The Android service will be used to listen to all the individual step details, using the step counter sensor, when the app is in the background. All the individual step details will be stored in the SQLite database, and finally the activity will be used to display the list of the total number of steps along with dates. Let's look at each component in detail:

1. The first component of our example is `StepsHistoryActivity`. We create a `ListView` in the activity to display the step count along with dates. Inside the `onCreate()` method of `StepsHistoryActivity`, we initiate `ListView` and `ListAdaptor`, which are required to populate the list. Another important task that we do in the `onCreate()` method is starting the service (`StepsService.class`), which will listen to all the individual steps events. We also make the call to the `getDataForList()` method, which is responsible for fetching the data for `ListView`. Inside the `getDataForList()` method, we initiate the object of the `StepsDBHelper` class and call the `readStepsEntries()` method of the `StepsDBHelper` class, which returns an `ArrayList` of the `DateStepsModel` objects containing the total number of steps along with dates after reading from the database:

```
public class StepsHistoryActivity extends Activity{

    private ListView mSensorListView;
    private ListAdapter mListAdapter;
    private StepsDBHelper mStepsDBHelper;
    private ArrayList<DateStepsModel> mStepCountList;

    @Override
    protected void onCreate(Bundle savedInstanceState){
    super.onCreate(savedInstanceState);
    setContentView(R.layout.activity_main);
    mSensorListView = (ListView)
    findViewById(R.id.steps_list);
    getDataForList();
    mListAdapter = new ListAdapter();
    mSensorListView.setAdapter(mListAdapter);
    Intent stepsIntent = new
    Intent(getApplicationContext(), StepsService.class);
    startService(mStepsIntent);
    }

    public void getDataForList(){
      mStepsDBHelper = new StepsDBHelper(this);
      mStepCountList = mStepsDBHelper.readStepsEntries();
    }
```

2. In our example, the `DateStepsModel` class is used as a **POJO** (Plain Old Java Object; it's a handy way of grouping logical data together) class to store the total number of steps and date. We also use the `StepsDBHelper` class to read and write the steps data in the database (this is discussed further in the next section). The `ListAdapter` class is used to populate the values for `ListView`, which internally uses `ArrayList` of `DateStepsModel` as a data source. The individual list item is the string, which is the concatenation of the date and total number of steps. Both the `DateStepsModel` class and the `ListAdapter` class are placed in a separate package in the code structure:

```java
public class DateStepsModel {

  public String mDate;
  public int mStepCount;
}


public class ListAdapter extends BaseAdapter {

  TextView mDateStepCountText;
  ArrayList<DateStepsModel> mStepCountList;
  Context mContext;
  LayoutInflater mLayoutInflater;
  public ListAdapter(ArrayList<DateStepsModel>
  mStepCountList, Context mContext) {
    this.mStepCountList = mStepCountList;
    this.mContext = mContext;
    this.mLayoutInflater =
    (LayoutInflater)this.mContext.getSystemService
    (Context.LAYOUT_INFLATER_SERVICE);
  }

  @Override
  public int getCount() {

    return mStepCountList.size();
  }

  @Override
  public Object getItem(int position) {

    return mStepCountList.get(position);
  }

  @Override
  public long getItemId(int position) {
```

```
        return position;
    }

    @Override
    public View getView(int position, View convertView,
    ViewGroup parent) {

      if(convertView==null){
       convertView = mLayoutInflater.inflate
       (R.layout.list_rows, parent, false);
      }

      mDateStepCountText =
      (TextView)convertView.findViewById
      (R.id.sensor_name);
      mDateStepCountText.setText
      (mStepCountList.get(position).mDate + " - Total
      Steps: " + String.valueOf(mStepCountList.get
      (position).mStepCount));

      return convertView;
    }
```

3. The second component of our example is `StepsService`, which runs in the background and listens to the step detector sensor until the app is uninstalled. In normal cases, when not required, you can stop the service using `stopService(new Intent(this,StepsService.class))` and unregister the `SensorEventListener`. We initiate the objects of `StepsDBHelper`, `SensorManager` and the step detector sensor inside the `onCreate()` method of the service. We only register the listener when the step detector sensor is available on the device. A point to note here is that we never unregister the listener because we expect our app to log the step information indefinitely, all the way until the app is uninstalled. Both the step detector and step counter sensors are very low on battery consumption and are highly optimized at the hardware level, so if the app really requires it, it can use them for longer durations without affecting the battery consumption much. We get a step detector sensor callback in the `onSensorChanged()` method whenever the operating system detects a step, and from it, we call the `createStepsEntry()` method of the `StepsDBHelper` class to store step information in the database:

```
public class StepsService extends Service implements
SensorEventListener{

    private SensorManager mSensorManager;
```

```
private Sensor mStepDetectorSensor;
private StepsDBHelper mStepsDBHelper;

@Override
public void onCreate() {
  super.onCreate();

  mSensorManager = (SensorManager)
  this.getSystemService(Context.SENSOR_SERVICE);
  if(mSensorManager.getDefaultSensor
  (Sensor.TYPE_STEP_DETECTOR) != null)
  {
    mStepDetectorSensor =
    mSensorManager.getDefaultSensor
    (Sensor.TYPE_STEP_DETECTOR);
    mSensorManager.registerListener(this,
    mStepDetectorSensor,
    SensorManager.SENSOR_DELAY_NORMAL);
    mStepsDBHelper = new StepsDBHelper(this);
  }
}

@Override
public int onStartCommand(Intent intent, int flags,
int startId) {
  return Service.START_STICKY;
}

@Override
public void onSensorChanged(SensorEvent event) {
mStepsDBHelper.createStepsEntry();
}
```

4. The last component of our example is the SQLite database. We create a StepsDBHelper class and extend it from the SQLiteOpenHelper abstract utility class provided by the android framework to easily manage the database operations. In the class, we create a database called StepsDatabase, which is automatically created on the first object creation of the StepsDBHelper class by the onCreate() method. This database has one table, StepsSummary, which consists of the following 3 columns (id, stepcount, and creationdate):

- The first column, id, is the unique integer identifier for each row of the table and is incremented automatically on the creation of every new row

- The second column, stepscount, is used to store the total number of steps taken on each date
- The third column, creationdate, is used to store the date in the mm/dd/yyyy string format

Inside the createStepsEntry() method, we first check if there is any existing step count with the current date, and if we find one existing, then we read the existing step count of the current date and update the step count by incrementing it by 1. If there is no step count with the current date found, then we assume that it is the first step of the current date and we create a new entry in the table with the current date and step count value as 1. The createStepsEntry() method is called from onSensorChanged() from the StepsService class whenever a new step is detected by the step detector sensor:

```
public class StepsDBHelper extends SQLiteOpenHelper
{

    private static final int DATABASE_VERSION = 1;
    private static final String DATABASE_NAME =
    "StepsDatabase";
    private static final String TABLE_STEPS_SUMMARY =
    "StepsSummary";
    private static final String ID = "id";
    private static final String STEPS_COUNT =
    "stepscount";
    private static final String CREATION_DATE =
    "creationdate";

    private static final String
    CREATE_TABLE_STEPS_SUMMARY = "CREATE TABLE "
    + TABLE_STEPS_SUMMARY + "(" + ID + " INTEGER
    PRIMARY KEY AUTOINCREMENT," +
    CREATION_DATE + " TEXT,"+ STEPS_COUNT + "
    INTEGER"+")";

    @Override
    public void onCreate(SQLiteDatabase db) {
    db.execSQL(CREATE_TABLE_STEPS_SUMMARY);
    }

    public boolean createStepsEntry() {

        boolean isDateAlreadyPresent = false;
        boolean createSuccessful = false;
        int currentDateStepCounts = 0;
        Calendar mCalendar = Calendar.getInstance();
```

```
String todayDate = String.valueOf(mCalendar
.get(Calendar.MONTH))+"/" +
String.valueOf(mCalendar.get
(Calendar.DAY_OF_MONTH)+1)+"/"+String.valueOf
(mCalendar.get(Calendar.YEAR));
String selectQuery = "SELECT " + STEPS_COUNT
+ " FROM " + TABLE_STEPS_SUMMARY + " WHERE "
+ CREATION_DATE +" = '"+ todayDate+"'";
try {
  SQLiteDatabase db = this.getReadableDatabase();
  Cursor c = db.rawQuery(selectQuery, null);
  if (c.moveToFirst()) {
    do {
      isDateAlreadyPresent = true;
      currentDateStepCounts =
      c.getInt((c.getColumnIndex(STEPS_COUNT)));
    } while (c.moveToNext());
  }
  db.close();
} catch (Exception e) {
  e.printStackTrace();
}
try {
  SQLiteDatabase db = this.getWritableDatabase();
  ContentValues values = new ContentValues();
  values.put(CREATION_DATE, todayDate);
  if(isDateAlreadyPresent) {
    values.put(STEPS_COUNT,
    ++currentDateStepCounts);
    int row = db.update(TABLE_STEPS_SUMMARY,
    values,  CREATION_DATE +" = '"+ todayDate+"'",
    null);
    if(row == 1) {
      createSuccessful = true;
    }
    db.close();
  } else {
    values.put(STEPS_COUNT, 1);
    long row = db.insert(TABLE_STEPS_SUMMARY,
    null, values);
    if(row!=-1) {
      createSuccessful = true;
    }
    db.close();
  }
} catch (Exception e) {
  e.printStackTrace();
}
```

```
    return createSuccessful;
}
```

5. The `readStepsEntries()` method is called from `StepsHistoryActivity` to display the total number of steps along with the date in `ListView`. The `readStepsEntries()` method reads all the step counts along with their dates from the table and fills the `ArrayList` of `DateStepsModel`, which is used as the data source for populating `ListView` in `StepsHistoryActivity`:

```java
public ArrayList<DateStepsModel> readStepsEntries()
{
  ArrayList<DateStepsModel> mStepCountList = new
  ArrayList<DateStepsModel>();
  String selectQuery = "SELECT * FROM " +
  TABLE_STEPS_SUMMARY;
  try {
    SQLiteDatabase db = this.getReadableDatabase();
    Cursor c = db.rawQuery(selectQuery, null);
    if (c.moveToFirst()) {
    do {
      DateStepsModel mDateStepsModel = new
      DateStepsModel();
      mDateStepsModel.mDate = c.getString
      ((c.getColumnIndex(CREATION_DATE)));
      mDateStepsModel.mStepCount = c.getInt
      ((c.getColumnIndex(STEPS_COUNT)));
      mStepCountList.add(mDateStepsModel);
    } while (c.moveToNext());
  }
  db.close();
} catch (Exception e) {
  e.printStackTrace();
}
  return mStepCountList;
}
```

The following is the screenshot of the pedometer utility app showing the total number of steps taken per day, along with the date, since the app was installed on the phone:

What just happened?

We created a small pedometer utility app that maintains the step history along with the dates using the step detector sensor. We used StepsHistoryActivity to display the list of the total number of steps along with their dates. StepsService is used to listen to all the steps detected by the step detector sensor in the background, and finally, the StepsDBHelper class is used to create and update the total step count for each date and to read the total step counts along with dates from the database.

Understanding the walking, jogging, and running signatures using the accelerometer sensor's data

The step counter and step detector sensors are really useful, but they fail to provide advanced information on steps, such as what the type of step was (running, jogging, or walking), and what the duration of each step was. For developing an advanced pedometer app or a health and fitness app, the duration and type of step is valuable information. As a learning exercise, we will develop our own algorithm to detect the type of step and the duration of each step. We will use the accelerometer sensor for our algorithm. The accelerometer sensor is the best sensor that can detect motion and acceleration acting on the phone during the walking process. The first step in developing the algorithm is to understand how a step looks on the accelerometer sensor. In the following section, we will be looking at the different signatures of walking, jogging, and running, as seen on the accelerometer sensor's data.

The walking signature using the accelerometer sensor

The accelerometer sensor gives the acceleration acting on the device, in the x, y, and z axes of the phone, and these acceleration values consists of two components: first is the gravity acting on each of the x, y, and z axes, and second is the acceleration produced by any user-generated motion acting on each of the x, y, and z axes. When a person is walking with the phone in his pocket, then both the gravity and user-generated acceleration values constantly change on the x, y, and z axes because of the walking motion and because of the change in the orientation of the phone with respect to the earth's frame of reference. We will be using the length of vector ($Sqrt(x*x+y*y+z*z)$), which is independent of the device's orientation, to track the walking motion. This length of vector, which is the square root of the sum of the squares of the acceleration acting on each axis, includes the standard 9.8 m/s^2 of gravitational acceleration on the phone. Now, let's look at the following graph, which shows the length of vector, that is, $Sqrt(x*x+y*y+z*z)$, on the y axis, and the time in hours, minutes, seconds, and milliseconds on the x axis on the graph. This is when the phone is kept still on a table:

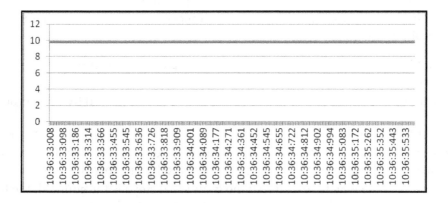

A point to note is that when the phone is kept still on a table, we only see the standard 9.8 m/s^2 of gravitational acceleration acting on the phone. Now, let's see what a normal walking signature looks like. The following graph shows the time on the *x* axis in hours, minutes, seconds, and milliseconds on the graph, while on the *y* axis, we have the length of vector. This is while the person is walking at a normal pace:

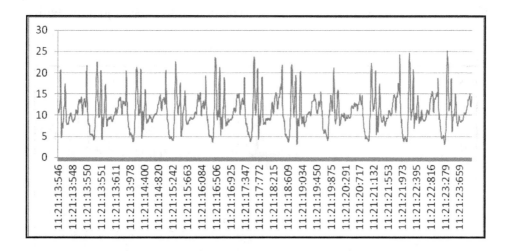

The preceding graph was plotted for 10 seconds of data, in which the user walked 10 steps, keeping his phone in the pocket of his pants. The following are a few important observations about the graph:

- All the individual steps generates a similar pattern, which repeats itself for each step
- The common pattern consists of a few high peaks followed by a few troughs
- Most of the time, the highest peak is registered when the foot hits on the ground
- The repeatable pattern, which can be used to separate one step from another, is that every step has one highest peak followed by one lowest trough
- One possible way to identify all the individual steps is the count all the highest peaks, each of which is followed by one lowest trough

The jogging or fast walking signature using the accelerometer sensor

Now, let's look at the following graph of a user who is walking fast or jogging with his phone in the pocket of his pants:

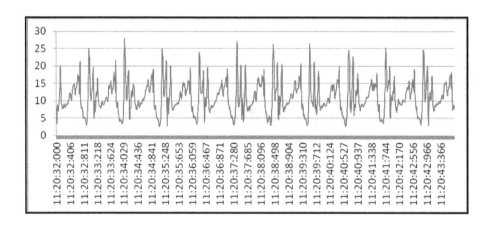

This graph looks very similar to the normal walking graphs, except for the following few differences:

- The highest peak value for normal walking reaches close to 20, while the highest peak for jogging or fast walking crosses 25.
- In the same time duration (that is, 10 seconds), the 11 highest peaks (steps) are noted. The time interval between each jogging step is shorter than ones in between the normal walking steps.

The running signature using the accelerometer sensor

Let's further analyze the graph of a user who is running with his phone in his pocket:

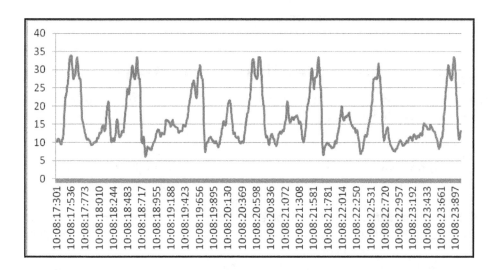

Now, let's analyze the differences of this running graph from the jogging and walking graphs. In this graph we see fewer peaks. Otherwise, it looks very similar to the normal walking graphs, except for the following few differences:

- The highest peak value for running crosses 30, while the highest peak for normal walking reaches close to 20, and the highest peak for jogging or fast walking doesn't cross 25.
- The time interval between running steps is shorter than the intervals between normal walking or jogging steps.

Every time we repeat the walking, jogging, and running tests and plot the data on graphs, we might get some variations in the pattern and values for the length of vector. There are many factors that can affect these patterns and length of vector, such as in which pocket the phone is kept (shirt pocket versus pant pocket), what kind of clothes you are wearing (loose or tight), what kind of shoes you are wearing (soft sole or hard sole), and so on. One common thing that doesn't change is the repetitive pattern of steps. Every step can be easily identified with its one highest peak point followed by its lowest trough.

The type of step detection algorithm

Now, we will use our analysis from the previous section to develop an algorithm to detect the type of steps (walking, jogging, or running). We observed, from the accelerometer data plotted on graphs, that every type of step (walking, jogging, and running) has a unique signature pattern. Every step registers a high variation in acceleration when the foot hits the ground. This high variation in acceleration is recorded as the highest peak in the graph when the length of vector is plotted against the time. This highest peak is followed by the lowest trough in the graph, and a pair comprising highest peak and lowest trough corresponds to a complete step. We will be extending the same logic in our algorithm to count the total number of steps. We will be identifying all the highest peaks, which are followed by lowest troughs, to get the total number of steps taken by the user. The difference in the magnitude of their highest peak values will help us differentiate between the types of steps. After experimentation with this algorithm, we found that the relative difference between peak values of running steps versus jogging steps is close to 5, and similarly, the relative difference between peak values of jogging steps versus walking steps is also approximately 5. We will be using this relative difference between the peaks to identify the type of step (walking, jogging, and running). The difference in peak values might vary depending on a lot of factors such as the ground, shoes, location of the phone, and so on.

Making it battery- and CPU-efficient using sensor fusion

The type of step detection algorithm using the accelerometer sensor has one major drawback. In order to work efficiently, it has to process the accelerometer sensor data all the time at the highest frequency, even when the phone is not in motion. This would consume a lot of battery and would keep the CPU engaged in sensor data processing forever. This shortcoming of algorithm can be resolved with the help of the step detector sensor. The step detector sensor is very low on battery consumption and is highly optimized on the hardware level. We will only start processing the accelerometer sensor data when we detect a step from the step detector sensor, and we will stop processing the accelerometer sensor data 20 seconds after the last step was detected. By combining two sensors, we will be able to process the accelerometer sensor data only when the user has actually taken steps, and this will make the algorithm highly battery- and CPU-efficient.

Scope for improvement

The whole purpose of this exercise is to learn and understand how the sensor's data can be used to develop algorithms, and how we can further improve them by adding more sensors (sensor fusion). That's why we have kept the algorithm simple and basic. The same type of step detection algorithm can be developed using various approaches. We can further improve the accuracy of the algorithm by adding advanced signal processing, digital filtering, and machine learning algorithms. The discussion and implementation of these advanced techniques are out of the scope of this book.

Time for action – type of step (walking, jogging, and running) detection using the accelerometer sensor

This section is dedicated to the implementation of the type of step detection algorithm discussed in the previous section. Our implementation for the algorithm will consist of four major components of android: first is android service, which will stay in the background, second is a set of two threads using the `ScheduledExecutorService`, and third is the activity to show the pedometer application data. The last component is the SQLite database to store the steps' information. The following is the high-level class diagram of the application; we will discuss each class in detail in their own sections. Now, let's explore the first component in detail:

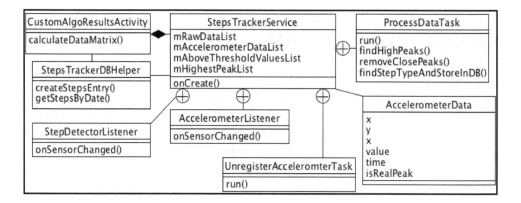

1. The first component of the algorithm is the `StepsTrackerService` service, which will remain in the background and provide a container for execution. Inside this service, we create the `StepDetectorListener` and `AccelerometerListener` classes and implement them with the `SensorEventListener` interface so that they can receive the sensor events. In the `onCreate()` method of the service, we initiate `SensorManager` and the step detector sensor object after checking its availability. We register the `StepDetectorListener` with `SensorManager` as soon as the service is created. As discussed earlier, in order to make the algorithm battery and CPU efficient, we will only register the accelerometer listener and start processing the data when any step is detected using the step detector sensor.

Hence, we only create the accelerometer `Sensor` object in the `onCreate()` method and wait for any step detection before creating the object of the `AccelerometerListener` and registering it with the `SensorManager`. We also create the object of the `StepsTrackerDBHelper` class, which is our SQLite database utility for handling all the database operations:

```
public class StepsTrackerService extends Service{

  private SensorManager mSensorManager;
  private Sensor mStepDetectorSensor;
  private Sensor mAccelerometerSensor;
  private AccelerometerListener
  mAccelerometerListener;
  private StepDetectorListener mStepDetectorListener;
  StepsTrackerDBHelper mStepsTrackerDBHelper;

  @Override
  public void onCreate() {
    super.onCreate();

    mSensorManager = (SensorManager)
    this.getSystemService(Context.SENSOR_SERVICE);
    if(mSensorManager.getDefaultSensor
    (Sensor.TYPE_STEP_DETECTOR) != null)
    {
      mStepDetectorSensor =
      mSensorManager.getDefaultSensor
      (Sensor.TYPE_STEP_DETECTOR);
      mStepDetectorListener = new
      StepDetectorListener();
      mSensorManager.registerListener
      (mStepDetectorListener, mStepDetectorSensor,
      SensorManager.SENSOR_DELAY_FASTEST);
    }
    if(mSensorManager.getDefaultSensor
    (Sensor.TYPE_ACCELEROMETER) != null)
    {
      mAccelerometerSensor =
      mSensorManager.getDefaultSensor
      (Sensor.TYPE_ACCELEROMETER);
    }
    mStepsTrackerDBHelper = new
    StepsTrackerDBHelper(this);
  }
```

2. The second component that plays an important part in developing the algorithm is a set of two threads using the `ScheduledExecutorService`. It is the system level Android thread executor service that provides the required number of threads from its available pool of threads for execution. We initiate the object of the `ScheduledExecutorService` with only two threads, using the `Executors.newScheduledThreadPool(2)` method, and we use it to schedule the execution of our two threads. The `ScheduledFuture` class instance is used to store the reference of the scheduled thread obtained by scheduling it using the `ScheduledExecutorService.schedule()` method.

The `ScheduledFuture` instance will also be used to cancel the execution of a scheduled thread using the `ScheduledFuture.cancel()` method. For the step detection algorithm, we use two threads: first is the `UnregisterAcceleromterTask` thread, which implements the runnable interface and is responsible for unregistering the accelerometer sensor, and second is `ProcessDataTask`, which also implements the runnable interface and is used to process the accelerometer data periodically. We use the `mScheduledUnregisterAccelerometerTask` instance of the `ScheduledFuture` class to store the reference of scheduled execution of the `UnregisterAcceleromterTask` thread, and similarly, we store the reference of the scheduled execution of the `ProcessDataTask` thread in `mScheduledProcessDataTask`, which is also the instance of the `ScheduledFuture` class.

As the first part to the logic, we want to only register the accelerometer listener and start processing the accelerometer data when we detect any steps and this is achieved inside the `onSensorChanged()` method of the `StepDetectorListener` class, where we create the object of `AccelerometerListener` and register it with `SensorManager`. We only register `AccelerometerListener` if it is has not been registered earlier, and we check this by using a Boolean variable called `isAccelerometerRegistered`. When the `AccelerometerListener` is registered, we make it true and when it unregisters inside the `run()` method `UnregisterAcceleromterTask` thread, we make it false.

Before registering, we also make sure that the mAccelerometerSensor is not null, that is, the accelerometer sensor is present on the device. Now, the second part of the logic is to unregister the accelerometer listener and stop processing the accelerometer data when no steps have been detected for the last 20 seconds. This is achieved by scheduling the execution of a new instance of the UnregisterAcceleromterTask thread after 20 seconds every time that a new step is detected, and cancelling the last scheduled execution of instance of the UnregisterAcceleromterTask thread, if present. This keeps on postponing the un-registration of the accelerometer listener until no step is detected for the last 20 seconds.

We use the isScheduleUnregistered Boolean variable to check whether there is any old scheduled execution instances of the UnregisterAcceleromterTask thread pending for execution; if yes, then we cancel its execution using the cancel() method of the mScheduledUnregisterAccelerometerTask. As soon as the UnregisterAcceleromterTask thread is scheduled for future execution, we make the isScheduleUnregistered Boolean variable true, and after the successful execution of the UnregisterAcceleromterTask thread, we make it false. Inside the run() method of the UnregisterAcceleromterTask thread, we also stop the processing of accelerometer data by stopping the execution of the ProcessDataTask thread using the cancel() method of mScheduledProcessDataTask, which stores its scheduled execution reference:

```
ScheduledExecutorService mScheduledExecutorService =
Executors.newScheduledThreadPool(2);
private ScheduledFuture
mScheduledUnregisterAccelerometerTask;
private ScheduledFuture mScheduledProcessDataTask;
private UnregisterAcceleromterTask
mUnregisterAcceleromterTask;
private ProcessDataTask mProcessDataTask;
private boolean isScheduleUnregistered = false;
private boolean isAccelerometerRegistered = false;

class StepDetectorListener implements
SensorEventListener{

  @Override
  public void onSensorChanged(SensorEvent event) {

    if(!isAccelerometerRegistered &&
    mAccelerometerSensor!=null)
```

```
      {
        mAccelerometerListener = new
        AccelerometerListener();
        mSensorManager.registerListener
        (mAccelerometerListener, mAccelerometerSensor,
        SensorManager.SENSOR_DELAY_FASTEST);
        isAccelerometerRegistered = true;
      }
      if(isScheduleUnregistered)
      {
        mScheduledUnregisterAccelerometerTask
        .cancel(true);
      }
      mUnregisterAcceleromterTask = new
      UnregisterAcceleromterTask();
      mScheduledUnregisterAccelerometerTask =
      mScheduledExecutorService.schedule
      (mUnregisterAcceleromterTask, 20000,
      TimeUnit.MILLISECONDS);
      isScheduleUnregistered = true;
    }
  }

  class UnregisterAcceleromterTask implements Runnable
  {

    @Override
    public void run() {
      isAccelerometerRegistered = false;
      mSensorManager.unregisterListener
      (mAccelerometerListener);
      isScheduleUnregistered = false;
      mScheduledProcessDataTask.cancel(false);
    }
  }
}
```

3. We create an `AccelerometerData` (POJO) class to hold the accelerometer data together. It has the float *x*, *y*, and *z* variables to hold the acceleration values on the *x*, *y*, and *z* axes. A double value holds the square root of the sum of the squares of the acceleration acting on all the three axes, and long time is used for storing the timestamp of the event. The Boolean variable `isTruePeak` is initiated to true and is helpful in finding the peak values corresponding to each step. (More on this in the next section). We create four instances of `ArrayList` on the `AccelerometerData` objects to process the accelerometer data.

Each of them will be discussed as we use them. In the
`AccelerometerListener` constructor, we schedule the periodic execution of
the `ProcessDataTask` thread to execute every 10 seconds with an initial delay of
10 seconds using the `scheduleWithFixedDelay()` method
of `ScheduledExecutorService`. The `ProcessDataTask` thread contains all the
logic needed to process the raw accelerometer data and find the type of steps
through it. Going back to `AccelerometerListener`, it's only responsible for two
tasks: the first is scheduling the period execution of the `ProcessDataTask`
thread, and the second is collecting the raw accelerometer data in
the `onSensorChanged()` method and storing it in `mAccelerometerDataList`,
which is the `ArrayList` of the `AccelerometerData` objects.

Now, let's discuss the `ProcessDataTask` thread in detail, which executes every
10 seconds and processes the last 10 seconds of accelerometer data, which is
stored in the `mAccelerometerDataList`. Inside the `run()` method of
the `ProcessDataTask` thread, the first task we do is copy all the elements of
the `mAccelerometerDataList` into a new `ArrayList`
of `AccelerometerData` objects called `mRawDataList`. After coping, we empty
the `mAccelerometerDataList` by calling its `clear()` method. This is done to
avoid the concurrent access of `mAccelerometerDataList` from
the `OnSensorChanged()` method of `AccelerometerListener`, which tries to
add values to it, and from the `ProcessDataTask` thread's `run()` method, which
reads values from it.

After this step, we calculate the square root of the sum of the squares of the
acceleration on the *x*, *y*, and *z* axes and store it in the double `value` variable using
a `for` loop, and we also update the `SensorEvent` timestamp to the current epoch
timestamp in milliseconds in the same loop. By default, the timestamp of
any `SensorEvent` is the time in nanoseconds from the system's boot time and not
the epoch time (also called the Unix timestamp). A simple way to convert it to
epoch time is to first divide the `SensorEvent` timestamp by 1,000,000 (to convert
from nanoseconds to milliseconds) and then add the offset value. The offset value
is the time in milliseconds from the start of the epoch time until the phone boot up
time, and this can be calculated by subtracting
the `SystemClock.elapsedtime()` from `System.currentTimeMillis()`. The
remaining steps are discussed in the next section:

```
class AccelerometerData {
  public double value;
  public float x;
  public float y;
  public float z;
```

```
  public long time;
  public boolean isTruePeak = true;
}

private long timeOffsetValue;
ArrayList<AccelerometerData> mAccelerometerDataList
= new ArrayList<AccelerometerData>();
ArrayList<AccelerometerData> mRawDataList = new
ArrayList<AccelerometerData>();
ArrayList<AccelerometerData>
mAboveThresholdValuesList = new
ArrayList<AccelerometerData>();
ArrayList<AccelerometerData> mHighestPeakList
= new ArrayList<AccelerometerData>();

class AccelerometerListener implements
SensorEventListener{

  public AccelerometerListener()
  {
    mProcessDataTask = new ProcessDataTask();
    mScheduledProcessDataTask =
    mScheduledExecutorService.scheduleWithFixedDelay
    (mProcessDataTask, 10000, 10000,
    TimeUnit.MILLISECONDS);
  }

  @Override
  public void onSensorChanged(SensorEvent event) {

    AccelerometerData mAccelerometerData = new
    AccelerometerData();
    mAccelerometerData.x = event.values[0];
    mAccelerometerData.y = event.values[1];
    mAccelerometerData.z = event.values[2];
    mAccelerometerData.time = event.timestamp;
    mAccelerometerDataList.add(mAccelerometerData);
  }
}

class ProcessDataTask implements Runnable {

  @Override
  public void run() {
  //Copy accelerometer data from main sensor array
  in separate array for processing
  mRawDataList.addAll(mAccelerometerDataList);
  mAccelerometerDataList.clear();
```

```
//Calculating the magnitude (Square root of sum of
squares of x, y, z) & converting time from nano
seconds from boot time to epoc time
timeOffsetValue = System.currentTimeMillis() -
SystemClock.elapsedRealtime();
int dataSize = mRawDataList.size();

for (int i = 0; i < dataSize; i++) {

  mRawDataList.get(i).value =
  Math.sqrt(Math.pow(mRawDataList.get(i).x, 2) +
  Math.pow(mRawDataList.get(i).y, 2) +
  Math.pow(mRawDataList.get(i).z, 2));
  mRawDataList.get(i).time =
  (mRawDataList.get(i).time/1000000L) +
  timeOffsetValue;
}

//Calculating the High Peaks
findHighPeaks();
//Remove high peaks close to each other which are
within range of 0.4 seconds
removeClosePeaks();
//Find the type of step (Running, jogging,
walking) & store in Database
findStepTypeAndStoreInDB();

mRawDataList.clear();
mAboveThresholdValuesList.clear();
mHighestPeakList.clear();
}
```

4. Until now, we have just been preparing the infrastructure required to write the step detection algorithm. In this section, we will write the core logic of the algorithm. As derived in the analysis of the step detection algorithm, we have to count the highest peaks above the walking threshold value, which corresponds to the highest acceleration registered on the accelerometer sensor when an individual step hits the ground. We can easily observe in the following graph that for every individual step, there is a corresponding highest peak, which is coupled with a lowest trough value. The algorithm simply boils down to counting the unique highest peak values (marked with a green circle), which are above the threshold value (plotted with the orange line), and coupling them with the lowest trough values (marked with a red circle).

In the algorithm, we also have to deal with the false positive values (marked with a yellow circle). These false positive values are registered very close to the highest peak values.

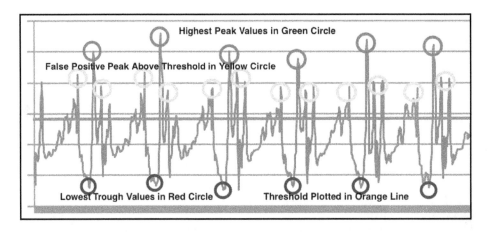

The first step in the algorithm is to find all the values that are above the walking threshold value and store them in `mAboveThresholdValuesListArrayList` of the `AccelerometerData` objects. We do this inside a `for` loop using the `if` condition, which is executed over the entire 10 seconds of accelerometer data stored in `mRawDataList`. The second step in the algorithm is to find all the potential highest peak values from the preceding threshold values. This is achieved by only adding above the threshold values in the `mAboveThresholdValuesList` until any value lower than the threshold value is received. As soon as any value lower than the threshold is found, we take the values collected thus far in the `mAboveThresholdValuesList` and sort them to find the highest potential peak among the values collected until that point that are above the threshold.

We use a custom `DataSorter` collection comparator class to sort the `mAboveThresholdValuesList` values. Now, this highest potential peak found among the above threshold values could be either a false positive (marked with a yellow circle in the figure), or a true highest peak value (marked with a green circle) corresponding to one step. We save this highest potential peak value in a separate `mHighestPeakListArrayList`. Before moving to the next group of above-threshold values, we clear all the data from the `mAboveThresholdValuesListArrayList`. After executing the `for` loop over the entire `mRawDataList`, we will get all the highest potential peaks, which consist of both false positive peak values (marked with the yellow circle in the figure) and the true highest peak values (marked with the green circle in the figure) in the `mHighestPeakList`.

Now, the third step of the algorithm is to filter out the false positive peak values from the true highest peak values. We know from the analysis of the data that these false positive values are pretty close to the true highest peak values, and also, their magnitude is less than the true highest peak's magnitude. We use the same logic in for loop to filter out the false positive values. We assume, by default, that all the values collected in the mHighestPeakList are true peaks. We do this using the Boolean variable, isTruePeak, in the AccelerometerData model class and initializing it to true. Inside for loop, we check the time difference between the two consecutive values; if the time difference is less than 0.4 seconds, then we assume that they are pretty close to each other and one of them is a false positive, and after this, we further compare their magnitude of length of vector, and whichever is smaller, we mark that value as a false positive.

After executing the for loop over the entire mHighestPeakList, we are able to filter out all the false positive values that have a lower magnitude and are near the highest peak values by setting their isTruePeak Boolean variable to false. Now, the final step in the algorithm is to detect the type of steps and save it in the database. This is done using a for loop over the mHighestPeakList inside the findStepTypeAndStoreInDB() method. Each type of step (running, jogging, and walking) is assigned a peak constant threshold value, which we have derived from the experimental data. For our algorithm, we are using the running peak value as 30, jogging peak value as 25, and walking peak value as 15. We execute a for loop only on those values of the mHighestPeakList that have the isTruePeak Boolean value as true. We categorize the elements of the mHighestPeakList by comparing the magnitude (length of vector) with the peak values of running, jogging, and walking, and also, we use the mStepsTrackerDBHelper.createStepsEntry() method to save the type and time of the step in the SQLite database:

```
public void findHighPeaks(){
    //Calculating the High Peaks
    boolean isAboveMeanLastValueTrue = false;
    int dataSize = mRawDataList.size();
    for (int i = 0; i < dataSize; i++)
    {
        if(mRawDataList.get(i).value > WALKINGPEAK)
        {
            mAboveThresholdValuesList.add
            (mRawDataList.get(i));
            isAboveMeanLastValueTrue = false;
        }
        else
        {
            if(!isAboveMeanLastValueTrue &&
```

```
        mAboveThresholdValuesList.size()>0)
        {
          Collections.sort(mAboveThresholdValuesList,
          new DataSorter());
          mHighestPeakList.add(mAboveThresholdValuesList
          .get(mAboveThresholdValuesList.size()-1));
          mAboveThresholdValuesList.clear();
        }
        isAboveMeanLastValueTrue = true;
      }
    }
  }

  public void removeClosePeaks()
  {
    int dataSize = mHighestPeakList.size();
      for (int i = 0; i < dataSize-1; i++) {

        if(mHighestPeakList.get(i).isTruePeak)
        {
          if(mHighestPeakList.get(i+1).time -
          mHighestPeakList.get(i).time < 400)
        {
          if(mHighestPeakList.get(i+1).value >
          mHighestPeakList.get(i).value)
          {
            mHighestPeakList.get(i).isTruePeak = false;
          }
          else
          {
            mHighestPeakList.get(i+1).isTruePeak = false;
          }
        }
      }
    }
  }

  public void findStepTypeAndStoreInDB()
  {
    int size = mHighestPeakList.size();
    for (int i = 0; i < size; i++)
    {
      if(mHighestPeakList.get(i).isTruePeak)
      {
        if(mHighestPeakList.get(i).value > RUNNINGPEAK)
        {
          mStepsTrackerDBHelper.createStepsEntry
          (mHighestPeakList.get(i).time, RUNNING);
```

```
    }
    else
    {
      if(mHighestPeakList.get(i).value > JOGGINGPEAK)
      {
        mStepsTrackerDBHelper.createStepsEntry
        (mHighestPeakList.get(i).time, JOGGING);
      }
      else
      {
        mStepsTrackerDBHelper.createStepsEntry
        (mHighestPeakList.get(i).time, WALKING);
      }
    }
  }
  }
}


public class DataSorter implements
Comparator<AccelerometerData>{

  public int compare(AccelerometerData obj1,
  AccelerometerData obj2){
    int returnVal = 0;

    if(obj1.value < obj2.value){
      returnVal =  -1;
    }else if(obj1.value > obj2.value){
      returnVal =  1;
    }
    return returnVal;
  }
}
```

5. We create a `StepsTrackerDBHelper` class to handle all the database operations and extend it from the Android SQLite built in the `SQLiteOpenHelper` utility class, which provides access to the database. Inside the class, we create a database called `StepsTrackerDatabase`, and it has only one table `StepsTrackerSummary`, which consists of the following four columns (`id`, `steptype`, `steptime`, and `stepdate`):

- The first column, `id`, is the unique integer identifier for each row of the table and is incremented automatically on the creation of every new row.
- The second column, `steptype`, is used to store the type of step (running, jogging, or walking).

- The third column is `steptime`, which is used to store the time in milliseconds.

- The fourth column is `stepdate`, which is used to store the date in the mm/dd/yyyy string format.

This class has a `createStepsEntry()` method that saves every step's information (the type, time, and date of every step) in a new row of the table. This method is called from `StepTrackerService` every time a new step is processed. There is another method of this class called `getStepsByDate()`, which is responsible for reading the total count of each type of step taken on a particular date, provided as the input parameter. This `getStepsByDate()` is called from the `CustomAlgoResultsActivity`, to display the pedometer data matrix. More on this in the next section:

```
public class StepsTrackerDBHelper extends SQLiteOpenHelper
{
  private static final String DATABASE_NAME =
  "StepsTrackerDatabase";
  private static final String TABLE_STEPS_SUMMARY =
  "StepsTrackerSummary";
  private static final String ID = "id";
  private static final String STEP_TYPE = "steptype";
  private static final String STEP_TIME = "steptime";//time is
  in milliseconds Epoch Time
  private static final String STEP_DATE = "stepdate";//Date
  format is mm/dd/yyyy

  private static final String CREATE_TABLE_STEPS_SUMMARY =
  "CREATE TABLE " + TABLE_STEPS_SUMMARY + "(" + ID + " INTEGER
  PRIMARY KEY AUTOINCREMENT," + STEP_DATE + " TEXT,"+
  STEP_TIME + " INTEGER,"+ STEP_TYPE + " TEXT"+")";

  public boolean createStepsEntry(long timeStamp, int
  stepType)
  {

    boolean createSuccessful = false;
    Calendar mCalendar = Calendar.getInstance();
    String todayDate =
    String.valueOf(mCalendar.get(Calendar.MONTH)+1)+"/" +
    String.valueOf(mCalendar.get(Calendar.DAY_OF_MONTH))+"/" +
    String.valueOf(mCalendar.get(Calendar.YEAR));
    try {
      SQLiteDatabase db = this.getWritableDatabase();
      ContentValues values = new ContentValues();
      values.put(STEP_TIME, timeStamp);
```

```
      values.put(STEP_DATE, todayDate);
      values.put(STEP_TYPE, stepType);
      long row = db.insert(TABLE_STEPS_SUMMARY, null, values);
      if(row!=-1)
      {
        createSuccessful = true;
      }
      db.close();

   } catch (Exception e) {
      e.printStackTrace();
   }
   return createSuccessful;
}

public int [] getStepsByDate(String date)
{
   int stepType[] = new int[3];
   String selectQuery = "SELECT " + STEP_TYPE + " FROM " +
   TABLE_STEPS_SUMMARY +" WHERE " + STEP_DATE +" = '"+
   date + "'";
   try {
      SQLiteDatabase db = this.getReadableDatabase();
      Cursor c = db.rawQuery(selectQuery, null);
      if (c.moveToFirst()) {
         do {
            switch(c.getInt((c.getColumnIndex(STEP_TYPE))))
            {
            case WALKING: ++stepType[0];
            break;
            case JOGGING: ++stepType[1];
            break;
            case RUNNING: ++stepType[2];
            break;
            }
         } while (c.moveToNext());
      }
      db.close();
   } catch (Exception e) {
      e.printStackTrace();
   }
   return stepType;
}

}
```

6. The last component of our application is to derive and display the pedometer data matrix (total steps, distance, duration, average speed, average step frequency, calories burned, and type of steps) on the user interface. We do this inside the `CustomAlgoResultsActivity` class. In the `onCreate()` method of the activity, we initiate seven instances of `TextView` to display the seven data matrix points (total steps, distance, duration, average speed, average step frequency, calorie burned, and type of steps). We also initiate the object of the `StepsTrackerDBHelper` class, which is used to read the steps' data from the database. The `calculateDataMatrix()` method, which is called from the `onCreate()` method and is responsible for calculating the data matrix and assigning the values to respective `TextView` on the user interface. Now, let's discuss how we can calculate each data point in the data matrix.

- The total numbers of steps are calculated by adding all the three types of steps (running, jogging, and walking) for a particular date. For our example, we use the current date for all the calculations. We use the `getStepsByDate()` method of the `StepsTrackerDBHelper` class to get the number of each type of step.
- The total number of each type of step is directly given by the `getStepsByDate()` method of the `StepsTrackerDBHelper` class, which returns the total number of each type of step in an integer array of capacity 3.
- The total distance is calculated by adding the distance travelled by all the three types of steps (running, jogging, and walking). With our experimental data, we found that walking a single step covers 0.5 meters, jogging a single step covers 1 meter, and running a single step covers close to 1.5 meters. Hence, we multiply the distance covered by each type of step with their respective numbers to get the total distance travelled.
- The total duration is also calculated by adding the time taken by all the three types of steps (running, jogging, and walking), and with the experimental sample data, we found that on average, a single walking step takes 1 second, a single jogging step takes 0.75 second, and a single running step takes 0.5 second. We multiply their individual step timings with the number of each type of step and add them together to get the total duration.
- We found that, on average, 1 calorie is burned by walking 20 steps (from various health resources such as `http://www.livestrong.com/article/320124-how-many-calories-does-the-average-person-use-per-step/`). Similarly, 1 calorie is burned by jogging 10 steps, and for running, 1 calorie is burned by five steps. Now, by multiplying the respective number of each step with the inverse of each number of steps required to burn 1 calorie, will give us the total number of calories burned.

- The average speed is calculated by dividing the total distance travelled by the total duration.
- The average step frequency is calculated by dividing the total number of steps taken by the total duration in minutes:

```java
public class CustomAlgoResultsActivity extends
Activity{
  private TextView mTotalStepsTextView;
  private TextView mTotalDistanceTextView;
  private TextView mTotalDurationTextView;
  private TextView mAverageSpeedTextView;
  private TextView mAveragFrequencyTextView;
  private TextView mTotalCalorieBurnedTextView;
  private TextView mPhysicalActivityTypeTextView;
  StepsTrackerDBHelper mStepsTrackerDBHelper;
  @Override
  protected void onCreate(Bundle savedInstanceState)
  {
    super.onCreate(savedInstanceState);
    setContentView(R.layout.capability_layout);
    mTotalStepsTextView =
    (TextView)findViewById(R.id.total_steps);
    mTotalDistanceTextView =
    (TextView)findViewById(R.id.total_distance);
    mTotalDurationTextView =
    (TextView)findViewById(R.id.total_duration);
    mAverageSpeedTextView =
    (TextView)findViewById(R.id.average_speed);
    mAveragFrequencyTextView =
    (TextView)findViewById(R.id.average_frequency);
    mTotalCalorieBurnedTextView =
    (TextView)findViewById(R.id.calories_burned);
    mPhysicalActivityTypeTextView =
    (TextView)findViewById
    (R.id.physical_activitytype);
    mStepsTrackerDBHelper = new
    StepsTrackerDBHelper(this);
    Intent mStepsAnalysisIntent = new
    Intent(getApplicationContext(),
    StepsTrackerService.class);
    startService(mStepsAnalysisIntent);
    calculateDataMatrix();
  }
  public void calculateDataMatrix()
  {
    Calendar mCalendar = Calendar.getInstance();
    String todayDate =
```

```
String.valueOf(mCalendar.get(Calendar.MONTH))
+"/" + String.valueOf(mCalendar.get
(Calendar.DAY_OF_MONTH)+1) +"/"+ String.valueOf
(mCalendar.get(Calendar.YEAR));
int stepType[] =
mStepsTrackerDBHelper.getStepsByDate(todayDate);
int walkingSteps = stepType[0];
int joggingSteps = stepType[1];
int runningSteps = stepType[2];
//Calculating total steps
int totalStepTaken = walkingSteps + joggingSteps
+ runningSteps;
mTotalStepsTextView.setText
(String.valueOf(totalStepTaken)+ " Steps");
//Calculating total distance travelled
float totalDistance = walkingSteps*0.5f +
joggingSteps * 1.0f + runningSteps * 1.5f;
mTotalDistanceTextView.setText
(String.valueOf(totalDistance)+" meters");
//Calculating total duration
float totalDuration = walkingSteps*1.0f +
joggingSteps * 0.75f + runningSteps * 0.5f;
float hours = totalDuration / 3600;
float minutes = (totalDuration % 3600) / 60;
float seconds = totalDuration % 60;
mTotalDurationTextView.setText
(String.format("%.0f",hours) + " hrs " +
String.format("%.0f",minutes) + " mins " +
String.format("%.0f",seconds)+ " secs");
//Calculating average speed
if(totalDistance>0)
{
  mAverageSpeedTextView.setText
  (String.format("%.2f",
  totalDistance/totalDuration)+" meter per
  seconds");
}
else
{
  mAverageSpeedTextView.setText
  ("0 meter per seconds");
}
//Calculating average step frequency
if(totalStepTaken>0)
{
  mAveragFrequencyTextView.setText
  (String.format("%.0f",totalStepTaken/minutes)+"
  steps per minute");
```

```
    }
    else
    {
      mAveragFrequencyTextView.setText
      ("0 steps per minute");
    }
    //Calculating total calories burned
    float totalCaloriesBurned = walkingSteps * 0.05f
    + joggingSteps * 0.1f + runningSteps * 0.2f;
    mTotalCalorieBurnedTextView.setText
    (String.format("%.0f",totalCaloriesBurned)+"
    Calories");

    //Calculating type of physical activity
    mPhysicalActivityTypeTextView.setText
    (String.valueOf(walkingSteps) + " Walking Steps "
    + "\n"+String.valueOf(joggingSteps) + " Jogging
    Steps " + "\n"+String.valueOf(runningSteps)+ "
    Running Steps");
}
```

The following is the screenshot of the pedometer app showing the pedometer data matrix (total steps, distance, duration, average speed, average step frequency, calories burned, and type of steps (walking, jogging, running)) active since the app was installed on the phone:

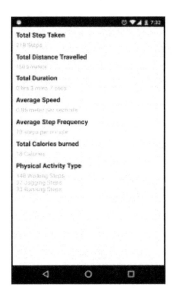

What just happened?

We did some really interesting developmental work for this pedometer application. First, we analyzed the accelerometer data to figure out the common pattern in the signatures of the walking, jogging, and running accelerometer sensor data. After that, we developed the type of step detection algorithm using this analysis. We also figured out how to use threads inside the service to process the accelerometer data in the background, and how to combine the step detector sensor with the accelerometer sensor to achieve battery optimization. We used our experimental data to derive the pedometer data matrix (total steps, distance, duration, average speed, average step frequency, calories burned, and type of steps) using the total number of each type of step detected by our algorithm.

Summary

We learned a lot of new concepts in this chapter, such as the step detector and step counter sensors. We learned how to develop the algorithm for detecting the types of steps (walking, jogging, fast running) using the accelerometer sensor data. We also looked at the infrastructure (service, threads, and database) required to process the sensor data in the background for a longer duration of time. This knowledge of the required infrastructure (service, threads, and database) will play an important role in developing efficient sensor-based applications.

7

The Google Fit Platform and APIs – The Fitness Tracker App

This chapter will introduce you to new ways of working with sensors. We will learn about the new Google Fit platform and how it can be used to manage fitness sensor data efficiently. We will explore the different APIs provided by the Google Fit platform. In this chapter, we will learn new concepts, such as how we can request the automated collection and storage of sensor data in a battery-efficient manner, without your app being in the background all the time. We will also learn how to get data from a remotely connected device, such as Android Wear. In this chapter, we will mostly deal with fitness sensors and as a learning exercise, we will develop a fitness tracker application that will collect and process your fitness data.

The topics you will learn about in this chapter are:

- What is the Google Fit platform?
- How the Android fitness APIs, Rest APIs and Google Fitness Store fit together into the Google Fit platform
- The details of six Android fitness APIs and the fundamentals of the Android fitness platform
- The user authorization process, required fitness scopes and permissions to use Android fitness APIs, and how to register your application with the Google developer console
- The implementation of Android fitness APIs inside the fitness tracker application, which will collect and process your fitness sensor data

- Getting the list of available fitness data sources on local or remotely connected devices and getting live fitness data from them
- Requesting the automated storage of fitness sensor data in a battery-efficient manner and retrieving fitness history data for a particular date range

The Google Fit platform

Google Fit is a platform that allows developers to manage user fitness data effectively. Developers, on behalf of users, can upload, download, and persist their fitness data to a central repository in the cloud. This fitness data can range from simple height and weight numbers to individual step information. The fitness data can come from various data sources, such as fitness apps, Android sensors, Android wear sensors or any other device that can connect and upload data to the Google Fit platform. The data sources can be present either locally on the phone or can be in remote devices in the form of any app or hardware sensors. This fitness data management is done using three key components, as shown in the following diagram: the first is the Google Fitness Store, which resides in the cloud; the second are web-based REST APIs; and the third are Android Fitness APIs which are on the Android devices. Now let's discuss each one of them separately in detail.

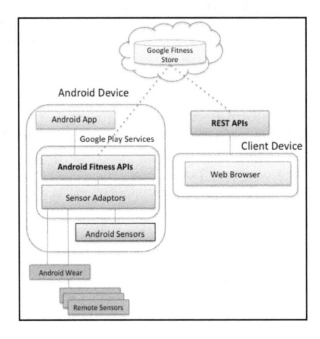

Google Fitness Store

All user fitness data is stored in the cloud on servers maintained by Google. Both REST APIs and Android Fitness APIs can manage data that is independently stored inside Google Fitness Store. If the user upgrades his Android phone, or removes any old fitness app or devices, then this data is persisted in the Google fitness store. This fitness data can be accessed from any platform, including Android, iOS or the Web, using one of these two APIs, but the user has to grant permission to the app before using either of these two APIs.

REST APIs

REST APIs are provided to support platforms other than Android. They can be used in an iOS native app or any web-based app. They are RESTful-based web services and use JSON for communications. They use the OAuth 2.0 protocol for authorization from users. REST APIs allow us to read, write and delete fitness data, but have some limitations when compared to Android Fitness APIs, such as not being able to discover fitness devices connected via Bluetooth and read their live sensor data streams. A detailed discussion and implementation of REST APIs is out of the scope of this book. We will mostly focus on Android Fitness APIs in this chapter.

Android Fitness APIs

Android Fitness APIs are part of Google Play Services, which comes as a part of the Android SDK. These APIs provide access to fitness data from two different sources: the first is a local source, which is any fitness Android app installed on the phone or any local sensor of the phone, while the second is a remote source, which is any fitness app or sensor installed on any other device. The Google Fitness platform doesn't differentiate between local or remote sources; it has its own categorization of data sources, which we will discuss in the coming sections. Android Fitness APIs can be used in Android applications after getting the required permissions from the user. They provide access to read, write, and delete fitness data. It also allows developers to create new fitness data types, scan for new **BLE (Bluetooth Low Energy)** fitness devices, and connect to them to get fitness data. There are six Android Fitness APIs to support this functionality. We will discuss each one of them in detail.

Sensors API

The Sensors API provides a list of available data sources that can provide live data streams. These data sources can be on a local device or on connected devices. It also allows the adding and removing of data listeners on a data source to read the live data stream coming from a sensor. This API is useful when we need to process live sensor fitness data. We will look at the implementation details in the fitness tracker application discussed in the second half of the chapter.

Recording API

The Recording API allows your app to request the automated storage of sensor data in a battery-efficient manner by creating subscriptions. A subscription is a form of request, which instructs the Recording API to save the data from different types of data sources or data types. It doesn't matter if your app is active or not; once a data type is subscribed successfully, it's the responsibility of the Google Fit platform to save the data of the requested data type until that data type is unsubscribed. The Recording API allows three major tasks: adding subscriptions, removing subscriptions, and listing active subscriptions. The data saved using Recording API subscriptions can be read using the History API. This API is useful when your app needs fitness data continuously in a battery-efficient manner and doesn't want to stay in the background forever to manage the storage of data.

History API

The History API allows your app to read, write, and delete fitness history data. It supports the batch importing of data from the fitness history. Through the History API, your app can read the data generated by any fitness app or sensor, but it can only delete the data generated by your own app. This API is useful when we need fitness data from any past date. We will look at the implementation details in the fitness tracker application discussed in the second half of the chapter.

Sessions API

Sessions are time intervals during which users perform any fitness activity, such as a run, a bike ride, or a game. Sessions help organize data and perform detailed or aggregate queries for a fitness activity. Sessions consist of a start time, an end time, a user-friendly name, a description, an activity type, and a unique identifier. Sessions do not contain fitness data themselves. Sessions can be considered as metadata objects with information that helps you query data from the fitness store later. The sessions API allows your app to create sessions in the fitness store using real-time data, or data you previously collected using the sensors API or from outside Google Fit. The API also allows your app to read, write, and delete the session data. This API is useful when we need to work with fitness metadata.

Bluetooth Low Energy API

The **Bluetooth Low Energy(BLE)** API allows your app to scan for any available BLE devices. Once a BLE device is found, the API also allows your app to claim the device. Once it's successfully claimed, the device can be used to get data via the Sensor API or Recording API. This API is useful when your app needs to connect to any new BLE device.

Config API

The Config API allows your app to create your own custom data type for your private app usage. This custom data type is not available to other apps. It also allows your app to retrieve shareable data types added by other apps or custom data types added by your app. This API is useful when there is no existing data type available that fits your needs and you want to create a new data type.

Platform basics

The following section explains the platform basics and fitness data formats and terminologies used by the Google Fit platform.

Data sources

Data sources represent unique sources of sensor data. They can expose raw data coming from hardware sensors on local or companion devices, which is categorized as `TYPE_RAW`. Data sources also expose derived data, created by transforming or merging other data sources, which are categorized as `TYPE_DERIVED`. They hold the metadata regarding the source, such as which hardware device (device name) or application (package name) generated the data. Multiple data sources can exist for the same data type, for example for the heart rate data type, we can have a heart rate sensor in a watch and a heart rate sensor in a chest wrap that show as two different data sources for one data type.

Data types

A data type defines the representation and format of any fitness data. It consists of a name and an ordered list of fields, where each field represents a dimension. For example, a data type for location contains three fields (latitude, longitude, and accuracy), whereas a data type for weight contains only one field. Certain data types can have corresponding aggregated data types; `AGGREGATE_STEP_COUNT_DELTA` is the aggregate data type of `TYPE_STEP_COUNT_DELTA`. For certain use cases, aggregated data types are very useful; for example, in a step counter application, a user would only be interested in knowing the total number of steps taken per day and not in the details (time) of each step. There are three kinds of data type:

- **Public data types**: These are the standard data types provided by the Google fit platform and can be used by every one.

- **Private custom data types**: These are custom data types that are specific to one app. Only the app that defines the data type can use it. They can be created using the Config API.

- **Sharable data types**: These are custom data types that are provided by third-party app developers and are approved by Google. Any app can read sharable data types, but only whitelisted apps, which are specified by a third-party developer, can write data of that sharable data type. For example, Nike and Adidas have made their sharable data types available for read only access. They can be read using the Config API.

Data point

A data point represents a single data point in a data type's stream from a particular data source. A data point holds a value for each field, a timestamp, and an optional start time. A single data point can have multiple fields and a single value for each field. A data point can hold an instantaneous measurement, reading, or inputted observation, as well as averages or aggregates over a time interval.

Data set

As the name suggests, this represents a set of data points of the same type from a particular data source covering a specific time interval. It is a grouping of data points based on a certain date or time range. We use datasets to insert data in, and read data from, the fitness store.

Authorization and permission scopes

User authorization is required before your application can read or write any fitness sensor data. User authorization is a two-step process. Step one is the registration of your application with the Google developer console, which is done outside your application. Step two is getting authorization from the user by using relevant scopes inside your application.

Registration with the Google developer console

Every application that needs to access fitness sensor data needs to register with the Google developer console. The followings steps explain the registration process:

1. Open the Google developer console in any browser.
2. Create a project from the console and enter your project name, which could be the same or different from your application name.
3. Find the **Fitness API** from the **APIs and Auth** console menu and turn it on. Now Fitness API should appear at the top of your API list.
4. Go to the **Credential** console menu and click on **Create a new Client ID**. This will open a new pop-up window to enter your application details into.
5. In the pop-up window, select your application type as **Android** and give the name of your application.

6. Provide the SHA1 fingerprint of your signing certificate in the relevant box of the pop-up window.
7. Provide the application package name from your manifest file and click on the **Create Client ID** button to complete the process.

Authorization from a user in the application

After completing the one-time registration with Google developer console, the user consent has to be taken inside the application. As a first step, we have to select the required scopes and then we have to connect to Google Play Services. Depending on the number of scopes set, Google Play Services will prompt the user with an authorization dialog showing the required permissions. Once the user gives consent, your applications can access the Fitness APIs. The implementation details are discussed in the fitness tracker application, in the second half of the chapter. The following is a screenshot of the authorization dialog, showing the required permissions for the device:

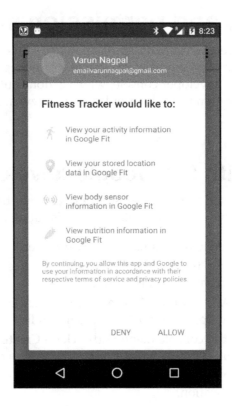

Fitness scopes

Scopes are strings that determine what kinds of fitness data an app can access and also define the level of access to this data. Scopes belong to a particular permissions group. The following table lists the different types of scope, their type of access, their data types, and the permissions group that they belong to.

Permission Group	Scopes	Type of Access	Data Types
Activity	FITNESS_ACTIVITY_READ	Read	com.google.activity.sample
			com.google.activity.segment
			com.google.activity.summary
			com.google.calories.consumed (deprecated)
			com.google.calories.expended
	FITNESS_ACTIVITY_READ_WRITE	Read and write	com.google.cycling.pedaling.cadence
			com.google.power.sample
			com.google.step_count.cadence
			com.google.step_count.delta
			com.google.activity.exercise
Body	FITNESS_BODY_READ	Read	com.google.heart_rate.bpm
			com.google.heart_rate.summary
	FITNESS_BODY_READ_WRITE	Read and write	com.google.height
			com.google.weight
			com.google.weight.summary
Location	FITNESS_LOCATION_READ	Read	com.google.cycling.wheel_revolution.cumulative
			com.google.cycling.wheel.revolutions
			com.google.distance.delta
	FITNESS_LOCATION_READ_WRITE	Read and write	com.google.location.sample
			com.google.location.bounding_box
			com.google.speed
			com.google.speed.summary
Nutrition	FITNESS_NUTRITION_READ	Read	com.google.nutrition.item
	FITNESS_NUTRITION_READ_WRITE	Read and write	com.google.nutrition.summary

Installing and running time permissions

If your application is using any of the `DataTypes` that belong to either the Location or Body permission groups shown in the preceding table, your application needs to have the following permissions:

- **Install time permissions in AndroidManifest.xml**: If your application uses a `DataType` that belong to either the Location or Body permission groups, then it needs to have `ACCESS_FINE_LOCATION` for Location-based data types and `BODY_SENSORS` for body-based data types.

- **Runtime permissions**: If your application uses a `DataType` that belong to either the Location or Body permission groups and is compiled with SDK version 23 (Marshmallow) or above, then your application needs to get run time permission for `ACCESS_FINE_LOCATION` and `BODY_SENSORS`.

The installation time permissions in `AndroidManifest.xml` and the run time permissions are different from the user authorization discussed in the previous section.

Fitness tracker app using fitness APIs

We have covered enough theory, now we will look at the implementation of these fitness APIs. As a learning exercise for this chapter, we will be developing a fitness tracker application that will make use of the fitness APIs we discussed so far in this chapter. This application will capture live fitness data and will also help users to track their fitness history. Let's explore the features and architecture of the application in detail.

Fitness tracker application requirements and architecture

The following list shows the high-level requirements of the fitness tracker application:

1. When the application starts for the first time, it should get the following authorizations from the user:
    1. To read their live fitness data with all the read scopes, using the Sensor API.
    2. To record their fitness data with all the read scopes, using Recording API.
    3. To read their fitness history data with all the read scopes, using History API.
2. The application should list all the available data sources for live data capture using the Sensors API.
3. The application should capture live data from available data sources. It should also allow adding and removing listeners using the Sensors API.
4. The application should list all the active subscriptions with their data types using the Recording API.
5. The application should allow adding and removing of subscriptions for a particular data type using the Recording API.

6. The application should show the history of available fitness data types from a selected date range to the user using the History API.
7. The application should show the aggregated history of available fitness data types by individual day, using the buckets filter provided by History API.

The following is the class diagram of the fitness tracker application, along with the high-level functionality of classes:

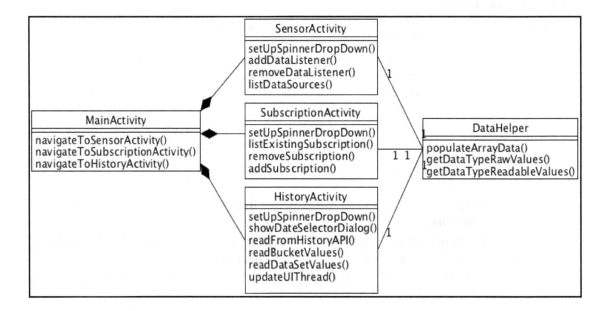

1. `SensorActivity`: This is an instance of Android activity and is responsible for listing the available data sources. It gets authorization from the user to read live fitness data. It also captures and displays live fitness data by adding a listener for a particular data type using Sensors API. It also removes a previously added listener.

2. `SubscriptionActivity`: This is an instance of Android activity and is responsible for listing all the active subscriptions. It also allows adding and removing of subscriptions for a particular data type using the Recording API.

3. `HistoryActivity`: This is an instance of Android activity and allows your app to query and aggregate the history of available fitness data types from a selected date range using History API and shows the results to the user.

4. `MainActivity`: This is an instance of Android activity and provides the first screen of the application. The sole purpose of this class is to navigate between the previous three activities.

5. `DataHelper`: This is a singleton data utility class that provides human readable strings for all the available data types in the form of `ArrayList<String>`. It also provides all the available data types in the form of `ArrayList<DataType>`.

Time for action – working with live fitness data using the Sensors API

The Sensors API is provided to work with a live stream of fitness sensor data. It can provide data from sensors on local or connected devices. The Sensors API is a part of Google play services and can be connected using the `GoogleApiClient` class. In `SensorActivity`, we first add the required scopes and Sensors API and then connect to Google play services using an object of the `GoogleApiClient` class. The steps for connecting to Google play services via the `GoogleApiClient` class are explained in the first section of the driving event detection application of the bonus chapter, *Sensor Fusion and Sensors-Based APIs – The Driving Events Detection App*, during the discussion on the activity recognition API. The only difference in steps is that, instead of adding activity recognition API; we have to add Sensors API. Now let's look at the individual tasks performed by `SensorActivity`:

1. The first task performed by `SensorActivity` is to get authorization from the user to read live fitness data using the Sensors API. This authorization only has to be requested the first time. To get authorization, we first create an object of the `GoogleApiClient` class in the activity's `onCreate()` method and then add the `Fitness.SENSORS_API` and relevant scopes in the object. To test all the available data sources, we add all the four possible scopes, but for a real-world application, we should only add the required scopes, as these scopes are visible to the user in the authorization system dialog. We also have to add the connection successful and failed callback listeners in the `GoogleApiClient` object. After creating the `GoogleApiClient` object, we connect it to the Google service library in activity's `onStart()` method and disconnect the `onStop()` method of the activity. If the user has already provided authorization, it will be connected successfully and will be notified through the `onConnected()` method callback.

But if the user has not given authorization before, then the connection will fail and will be notified through the onConnectionFailed() method callback. If the connection failed because of non-authorization, or any other reason that can be resolved by Google play services, then the method hasResolution() of the ConnectionResult object inside the onConnectionFailed() method is passed as true and we can call the startResolutionForResult() method of the ConnectionResult object. This will present the user with the authorization system dialog asking for relevant permissions if the user has not provided these permissions before. If there is any other reason for the connection to fail, such as the user doesn't have a fitness account or it is not configured, then it will try to resolve that. Once the user has given permission, it will notified in the onActivityResult() method with the same request code that we requested in the startResolutionForResult() method, and from there we can again try to connect to Google services:

```
public class SensorActivity extends Activity
implements ConnectionCallbacks,
OnConnectionFailedListener, OnItemSelectedListener,
OnItemClickListener{

@Override
protected void onCreate(Bundle savedInstanceState) {
  super.onCreate(savedInstanceState);
  setContentView(R.layout.livedata_layout);
  mLiveDataText =
  (TextView)findViewById(R.id.livedata);

  setUpSpinnerDropDown();
  setUpListView();

  mClient = new GoogleApiClient.Builder(this)
  .addApi(Fitness.SENSORS_API).addScope(new
  Scope(Scopes.FITNESS_ACTIVITY_READ))
  .addScope(new Scope(Scopes.FITNESS_BODY_READ))
  .addScope(new Scope(Scopes.FITNESS_LOCATION_READ))
  .addScope(new Scope(Scopes.FITNESS_NUTRITION_READ))
  .addConnectionCallbacks(this)
  .addOnConnectionFailedListener(this).build();
}

@Override
public void onConnectionFailed(ConnectionResult
connectionResult) {

  if(connectionResult.hasResolution()){
```

```
    try {
      connectionResult.startResolutionForResult
      (SensorActivity.this, REQUEST_OAUTH);
    }catch (Exception e)
    {
      e.printStackTrace();
    }
  }
}

@Override
protected void onActivityResult(intrequestCode,
intresultCode, Intent data) {
  if (requestCode == REQUEST_OAUTH&&resultCode ==
  RESULT_OK) {
    if (!mClient.isConnecting() &&
    !mClient.isConnected()) {
      mClient.connect();
    }
  }
}
```

2. The second important task performed by `SensorActivity` is to list all the available data sources for a selected data type. We use the spinner drop-down to let the user select a particular data type. In the `setUpSpinnerDropDown()` method, we set up the spinner and set it on the selected listener. We get all the human readable string values for all the available data types from the `getDataTypeReadableValues()` method of the `DataHelper` utility singleton class. After the user has selected a data type from the spinner drop-down value, we find all its available data sources. In the `onItemSelected()` spinner callback, we get the selected item position, and by using the `getDataTypeRawValues()` method of the `DataHelper` utility class, we get its corresponding `DataType` object value, which is then passed to the `listDataSources()` method to query the available data sources. Inside the `listDataSources()` method, we use the `findDataSources()` method of the `Fitness.SensorsApi` class to query all the available data sources.

The findDataSources() API requires two parameters: the first is the object of GoogleApiClient and the second is the object of DataSourcesRequest, which has a builder syntax shown in the following code snippet.

The DataSourcesRequest API accepts two parameters: the first is the data type, which is a mandatory parameter, and second is the type of data source (TYPE_DERIVED and TYPE_RAW), which is an optional parameter. If we don't specify the type of data sources, then we will receive both types of data source. The result of the available data sources is received inside the result listener, which is set by passing the object of ResultCallback<DataSourcesResult> inside the setResultCallback() method of the findDataSources() API. The result is received in the form of List<DataSource>, which contains all the available DataSource objects for that particular data type. Using this list, we populate our local mDataSourceList, which is the ArrayList of DataSource. We show the entire list of available data sources in the ListView, which is set up inside the setUpListView() method and is called from the onCreate() method of the activity. If no data source is found, then we display the relevant message in mLiveDataText, which is the object of TextView. We set the item click listener on the ListView to receive the index of the clicked data source item for which the data listener will be added (this is explained in the next section). The implementation details of ListAdapter can be found in the code that comes with this chapter:

```
public void setUpListView() {

  mListView =
  (ListView)findViewById(R.id.datasource_list);
  mListAdapter = new ListAdapter();
  mListView.setOnItemClickListener(this);
  mListView.setAdapter(mListAdapter);
}

public void setUpSpinnerDropDown() {

  Spinner spinnerDropDown = (Spinner)
  findViewById(R.id.spinner);
  spinnerDropDown.setOnItemSelectedListener(this);
  ArrayAdapter<String> arrayAdapter = new
  ArrayAdapter<String>(this,
  android.R.layout.simple_spinner_item,
  DataHelper.getInstance()
  .getDataTypeReadableValues());
  arrayAdapter.setDropDownViewResource
  (android.R.layout.simple_spinner_dropdown_item);
  spinnerDropDown.setAdapter(arrayAdapter);
```

```
    }

    public void listDataSources(DataType mDataType)
    {
      Fitness.SensorsApi.findDataSources(mClient, new
      DataSourcesRequest.Builder().setDataTypes(mDataType)
      .setDataSourceTypes(DataSource.TYPE_DERIVED)
      .setDataSourceTypes(DataSource.TYPE_RAW).build())
      .setResultCallback(new
      ResultCallback<DataSourcesResult>() {
        @Override
        public void onResult(DataSourcesResult
        dataSourcesResult) {
          mListAdapter.notifyDataSetChanged();
          if (dataSourcesResult.getDataSources()
          .size() > 0) {
          mDataSourceList.addAll
          (dataSourcesResult.getDataSources());
          mLiveDataText.setText("Please select from
          following data source to get the live data");
          } else {
            mLiveDataText.setText("No data source found
            for selected data type");
          }
        }
      });
    }


    @Override
    public void onItemSelected(AdapterView<?> parent, View
    view, int position, long id) {

      if (mClient.isConnected() && position!=0) {
        listDataSources(DataHelper.getInstance()
        .getDataTypeRawValues().get(position));
        if(mDataSourceList.size()>0) {
          mDataSourceList.clear();
        }
      }
    }
```

3. After getting the available data sources for a particular data type, we can get the live data from the data source. To get the live data from the data source, we have to add the object of `OnDataPointListener`. In our example, we first get the clicked position of the data source item of the `ListView` inside the `onItemClick()` method and, using the position, we get the corresponding `DataSource` object from `mDataSourceList` and pass this object to the `addDataListener()` method for adding the listener. Inside the `addDataListener()` method, we use the `add()` method of the `Fitness.SensorsApi` class to add the listener and get the live sensor data. The `add()` API requires three parameters: the first is the object of `GoogleApiClient` and the second is the object of `SensorRequest`, which has a builder syntax shown in the following code snippet. The API accepts three important parameters: the first one is the sampling rate, the second is the mandatory data type, and the third parameter is the optional data source in the `SensorRequest` object. Another parameter accepted by the `add()` API is the object of `OnDataPointListener`, which receives the live data from sensors and returns it in the form of a single `DataPoint` object. The `DataPoint` object consists of multiple fields and their values. For our example, we iterate over all the fields and their values using a `for` loop and show them in the `mLiveDataText` label. The `add()` API also allows us to set the result callback by passing the object of `ResultCallback<Status>` inside the `setResultCallback()` method of the API. Depending on the status received in this result callback, we set the relevant message in the `mLiveDataText` label. Before adding the data point listener, we check if there is an existing listener already added by using the `isDataListenerAdded` Boolean variable inside the `onItemClick()` method. If the data point listener has already been added, then we remove it by calling the `removeDataListener()` method. Inside the `removeDataListener()` method, we remove the existing data point listener using the `remove()` method of the `Fitness.SensorsApi` class. It accepts two arguments: the first is the object of `GoogleApiClient` and the second is the object of the existing data point listener. We set the `isDataListenerAdded` Boolean variable back to `false` after the successful removal of the listener:

```
@Override
public void onItemClick(AdapterView<?> parent, View
view, int position, long id) {

    //remove any existing data listener,if previously
    added.
    if(isDataListenerAdded) {
```

```
      removeDataListener();
    }
    addDataListener(mDataSourceList.get(position));
  }

public void addDataListener(DataSource mDataSource)
{
  Fitness.SensorsApi.add(mClient, new
  SensorRequest.Builder().setDataSource(mDataSource)
  .setDataType(mDataSource.getDataType())
  .setSamplingRate(1, TimeUnit.SECONDS)
  .build(), mOnDataPointListener)
  .setResultCallback(new ResultCallback<Status>() {
    @Override
    public void onResult(Status status) {
      if (status.isSuccess()) {
        mLiveDataText.setText("Listener registered
        successfully, waiting for live data");
        isDataListenerAdded = true;
      } else {
        mLiveDataText.setText("Listener registration
        failed");
      }
    }
  });
}

OnDataPointListener mOnDataPointListener = new
OnDataPointListener() {
  @Override
  public void onDataPoint(DataPoint dataPoint) {
    final StringBuilder dataValue = new
    StringBuilder();
    for (Field field :
    dataPoint.getDataType().getFields())
    {
      Value val = dataPoint.getValue(field);
      dataValue.append("Name:" + field.getName() + "
      Value:" + val.toString());
    }

    runOnUiThread(new Runnable() {
      @Override
      public void run() {
        mLiveDataText.setText(dataValue.toString());
      }
    });
  }
```

```
        };

        public void removeDataListener()
        {
          Fitness.SensorsApi.remove(mClient,
          mOnDataPointListener).setResultCallback(new
          ResultCallback<Status>() {
            @Override
            public void onResult(Status status) {
              if (status.isSuccess()) {
                isDataListenerAdded = false;
                Log.i(TAG, "Listener was remove
                successfully");
              } else {
                Log.i(TAG, "Listener was not removed");
              }
            }
          });
        }
```

What just happened?

We created a small utility that lists all the available data sources for a particular selected data type. For simplicity, we loaded all available names of data types in a spinner drop-down to select from. Once a data type is selected from the spinner drop-down, we load the available data sources in a list corresponding to that data type. A data type can have multiple data sources available from local or connected devices. Once any data source is clicked on from the list of available data sources, we add its listener and display the live data coming from that data source in a text field. This utility can be used in any use case where you have to process live sensor data. There are only a few data types, such as steps or location-based data types, for which you will find available data sources that provide live sensor data.

Most data sources provide data to the fitness store after processing. An important sensor that you would expect to provide live data is the heart rate BPM, especially on Android wear, but most Android wear (such as Moto 360 and LG Watch Urban), don't support the streaming of heart rate data over Bluetooth; instead they process the heart rate locally on the watch and upload it later to the Google Fitness Store. There are some chest wrap heart rate monitor devices, such as the Polar h7 Bluetooth heart rate sensor, that support the live streaming of heart rate data over Bluetooth. The following is a screenshot from a Nexus 5X device, showing the available data sources for the data type STEP COUNT DELTA:

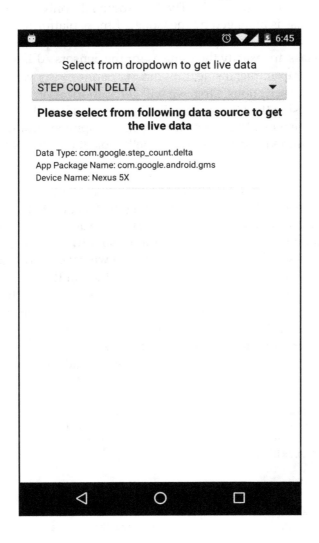

Time for action – recording fitness data in background using Recording API

The Recording API allows your app to request automated storage of sensor data in a battery-efficient manner by creating subscriptions. Once you add a subscription for a data type, then it's Google Play services' responsibility to start recording the data for the requested data type in the background. This recorded data is stored in the Google fitness store and can be queried by History API. The Recording API only decides which data type to record; everything else is managed by the Google fitness platform. The Recording API is part of Google play services. The steps for connecting to Google play services via the GoogleApiClient class are exactly the same as for the Sensors API, discussed in the previous section. In our example, inside SubscriptionActivity we will perform four important tasks with subscriptions. First, we will get authorization to read history data from the fitness store using the History API. Second, we will list all the existing subscriptions. Third, we will add subscriptions from the spinner drop-down. Finally, we will delete an already added subscription. Now let's look at the individual tasks performed by SubscriptionActivity:

1. The first task performed by SubscriptionActivityis to get authorization from the user to read history fitness data using the History API. This authorization has to be requested for the first time only. The code and process for getting authorization is exactly the same as for Sensors API, which we discussed in the previous section. The only difference is that we have to add RECORDING_API in place of SENSORS_API in the addApi() method of the GoogleApiClient class.Even though authorization has already been given in the SensorActivity class, we still have to get authorization for two reasons: we are using a different API (History API) and the user might go directly to SubscriptionActivity instead of going to SensorActivity first. The code used inSubscriptionActivity can be downloaded from the code bundle for this chapter:

```
public class SubscriptionActivity extends Activity
implements ConnectionCallbacks,
OnConnectionFailedListener, OnItemSelectedListener,
OnItemClickListener {

    @Override
    protected void onCreate(Bundle savedInstanceState) {
        super.onCreate(savedInstanceState);
        setContentView(R.layout.subscriptiondata_layout);

        mClient = new GoogleApiClient.Builder(this)
```

```
            .addApi(Fitness.RECORDING_API)
            .addScope(new Scope(Scopes.FITNESS_ACTIVITY_READ))
            .addScope(new Scope(Scopes.FITNESS_BODY_READ))
            .addScope(new Scope(Scopes.FITNESS_LOCATION_READ))
            .addScope(new
            Scope(Scopes.FITNESS_NUTRITION_READ))
            .addConnectionCallbacks(this)
            .addOnConnectionFailedListener(this).build();
        setUpSpinnerDropDown();
        setUpListView();
}
```

2. The second task performed by `SubscriptionActivity`is to list all the existing active subscriptions. We show the entire active subscriptions list of the data type in the `ListView`, which is set up inside the `setUpListView()` method (this method is the same as in the previous `SensorActivity` class) and is called from the `onCreate()` method of the activity. As soon as we get connected to the Google play services through the `GoogleApiClient` object, we call the `listExistingSubscription()`method to get the list of active subscriptions. Inside the `listExistingSubscription()`method, we use the `listSubscriptions()` method of Recording API to get the list of all active subscriptions asynchronously inside the object of `ResultCallback<ListSubscriptionsResult>`, which is set using the `setResultCallback()` method of the API. We receive a list of *Subscription* objects, which contains all the details of the active subscription. To display the results in the `ListView`, we only take the data type of the subscription and add it to the `mDataTypeList`, which acts a source for the `ListView`. We set the item click listener on the `ListView` to receive the clicked subscription item index. The implementation details of `ListAdapter` can be found in the code that comes with this chapter:

```
@Override
public void onConnected(Bundle bundle) {

    listExistingSubscription();
}

public void listExistingSubscription() {

    Fitness.RecordingApi.listSubscriptions(mClient)
    setResultCallback(new
    ResultCallback<ListSubscriptionsResult>() {
        @Override
        public void onResult(ListSubscriptionsResult
```

```
      listSubscriptionsResult) {
        mDataTypeList.clear();
        for (Subscription sc :
        listSubscriptionsResult.getSubscriptions()) {
          mDataTypeList.add(sc.getDataType());
        }
        runOnUiThread(new Runnable() {
          @Override
          public void run() {
            mListAdapter.notifyDataSetChanged();
          }
        });
      }
    });
  }
```

3. The third important task performed by `SubscriptionActivity`is to add
   subscriptions. We can add subscriptions based either on a data source or a data
   type. For our example, we add it using a data type. We use the spinner drop-
   down to let the user select a particular data type. In the
   `setUpSpinnerDropDown()` method (this method is the same as in the
   previous `SensorActivity` class) we set up the spinner and set its selected
   listener. We get all the human readable strings values for all the available data
   types from the `getDataTypeReadableValues()` method of the `DataHelper`
   utility singleton class. After the user has selected a data type from the spinner
   drop-down value, we add the subscription for that particular data type. In the
   `onItemSelected()` spinner callback, we get the selected item position and by
   using the `getDataTypeRawValues()` method of the `DataHelper` utility class,
   we get its corresponding `DataType` object value, which is then passed to the
   `addSubscription()` method for adding a subscription. Inside the
   `addSubscription()`method, we use the `subscribe()`method of Recording
   API to add the subscription. Once the subscription is successfully added, then we
   refresh the active subscription list by calling the
   `listExistingSubscription()` method:

```
@Override
public void onItemSelected(AdapterView<?> parent, View
view, int position, long id) {

  if(position!=0 && mClient.isConnected()) {
    addSubscription(DataHelper.getInstance()
    .getDataTypeRawValues().get(position));
  }
}
```

```
public void addSubscription(DataType mDataType) {
  Fitness.RecordingApi.subscribe(mClient, mDataType)
  .setResultCallback(new ResultCallback<Status>() {
    @Override
    public void onResult(Status status) {
      if (status.isSuccess()) {
        listExistingSubscription();
      } else {
        Log.i(TAG, "There was a problem subscribing.");
      }
    }
  });
}
```

4. The fourth and final task performed by SubscriptionActivityis to remove any active subscriptions. This is done by taking the clicked index of displayed active subscription data types on ListView inside onItemClick() and sending the corresponding data type to the removeSubscription() method. Inside the removeSubscription() method, we use the unsubscribe() method of Recording API to remove the active subscription. The unsubscribe() API accepts the object of the GoogleApiClient class and the data type to be removed. Once the subscription has been removed successfully, we remove the subscribed data type from mDataTypeList and refresh the ListView:

```
@Override
public void onItemClick(AdapterView<?> parent, View
view, int position, long id) {

  removeSubscription(mDataTypeList.get(position));
}

public void removeSubscription(DataType mDataType) {
  Fitness.RecordingApi.unsubscribe(mClient, mDataType)
  .setResultCallback(new ResultCallback<Status>() {
    @Override
    public void onResult(Status status) {
      if (status.isSuccess()) {
        runOnUiThread(new Runnable() {
          @Override
          public void run() {
            mDataTypeList.remove
            (lastRemovedPosition);
            mListAdapter.notifyDataSetChanged();
          }
        });
      } else {
```

```
            Log.i(TAG, "Failed to unsubscribe ");
        }
    }
});
}
```

What just happened?

In the `SubscriptionActivity`, we developed a utility that deals with all the operations (adding, removing, listing) for subscriptions. Subscriptions are really helpful when you don't want your application to manage the collection and storage of fitness data by staying in the background forever. All subscribed data is collected and stored in the Google Fitness Store and can be retrieved using History API, which we will discuss in the next section. The following is a screenshot from a Nexus 5X device showing the list of active subscriptions:

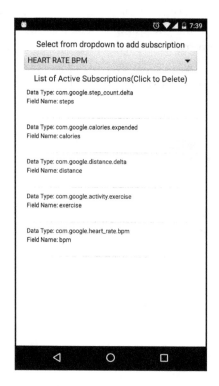

Time for action – getting history fitness data using the History API

We have seen in the previous section how to request the automated collection of fitness sensor data, now in this section we will learn how to retrieve all the collected data from the Google fitness store. The History API not only allows your application to retrieve fitness sensor data, but it also allows your app to write and delete fitness data. Your application can only delete the fitness data created by your own app. The History API provides an efficient way of querying fitness data and also supports the batch importing of data. The History API is part of Google Play services and follows the same process to connect as Sensors API or Recording API. In our example, we will focus on how to query the fitness data between two dates and get fitness data that is aggregated by day. We will let the user select the data type from the spinner drop-down, and select the start and end dates and the time picker. Users can also request to aggregate the data by using a check box in the user interface. Now let's look at the implementation details of the HistoryActivity class.

1. The first task performed by HistoryActivity is to take the relevant authorization for History API and scopes and connect to Google Play services. These steps are exactly the same as Sensors API or Recording API, so we will skip the explanation and move to the next section. The code used in HistoryActivity can be downloaded from the code bundle for this chapter:

```
public class HistoryActivity extends Activity
implements ConnectionCallbacks,
OnConnectionFailedListener, OnItemSelectedListener{

@Override
protected void onCreate(Bundle savedInstanceState) {
  super.onCreate(savedInstanceState);
  setContentView(R.layout.historydata_layout);

  mClient = new GoogleApiClient.Builder(this)
  .addApi(Fitness.HISTORY_API)
  .addScope(new Scope(Scopes.FITNESS_ACTIVITY_READ))
  .addScope(new Scope(Scopes.FITNESS_BODY_READ))
  .addScope(new Scope(Scopes.FITNESS_LOCATION_READ))
  .addScope(new Scope(Scopes.FITNESS_NUTRITION_READ))
  .addConnectionCallbacks(this)
  .addOnConnectionFailedListener(this).build();

  setUpSpinnerDropDown();
  setUpListView();
```

```
    mAggregateCheckBox =
    (CheckBox)findViewById(R.id.aggregatecheckbox);
    mStartDateText =
    (TextView)findViewById(R.id.startdate);
    mEndDateText = (TextView)findViewById(R.id.enddate);
    mResultsText = (TextView)findViewById(R.id.results);
}
```

2. The second task performed by `HistoryActivity` is to take input from the user interface for a selected data type, date interval, and aggregate condition. We let the user select the data type from the spinner drop-down, which is set up inside the `setUpSpinnerDropDown()` method. We receive the selected data type from the spinner drop-down inside the `onItemSelected()` method. We use `mAggregateCheckBox` to get the aggregate by day condition from the user and assign that value to the `isDataAggregated` Boolean variable. We use a custom dialog box to show the date and time picker. We take the start and end date values, and assign them to `mStartDateCalendar` and `mEndDateCalendar`, which are objects of the `Calendar` class. Once the user has selected the start date, end date, and aggregated condition from the user interface, we fire the query inside an `AsyncTask` object, which is an operating system-managed background thread, discussed in the next section. Following the screenshot of the custom date dialog created by `showDateSelectorDialog()` method.

```java
@Override
public void onItemSelected(AdapterView<?> parent, View
view, int position, long id) {
  if(position!=0) {
    mSelectedDataType = DataHelper.getInstance()
    .getDataTypeRawValues().get(position);
  }
}

public void setStartDate(View v) {
  showDateSelectorDialog(true);
}

public void setEndDate(View v) {
  showDateSelectorDialog(false);
}

public void showDateSelectorDialog(final boolean
isStartDate){

  final Dialog dialog = new Dialog(this);
  View view = LayoutInflater.from(this).inflate
```

```
(R.layout.date_time_layout, null, false);
dialog.setContentView(view);
dialog.setTitle("Select the Date and Time");
Button submit = (Button)
view.findViewById(R.id.submit);
Button cancel = (Button)
view.findViewById(R.id.cancel);

final TimePicker timePicker = (TimePicker)
view.findViewById(R.id.timepicker);
final DatePicker datePicker = (DatePicker)
view.findViewById(R.id.datepicker);

submit.setOnClickListener(new View.OnClickListener()
{

  @Override
  public void onClick(View arg0) {

    int hour = timePicker.getCurrentHour();
    int min = timePicker.getCurrentMinute();
    int month = datePicker.getMonth();
    int date = datePicker.getDayOfMonth();
    int year = datePicker.getYear();
    Calendar calendar = Calendar.getInstance();
    calendar.set(year, month, date, hour, min);
    if (isStartDate) {
      mStartDateCalendar = calendar;
      mStartDateText.setText(" Start Date: " +
      mSimpleDateFormat.format
      (mStartDateCalendar.getTime()));
    } else {
      mEndDateCalendar = calendar;
      mEndDateText.setText(" End Date: " +
      mSimpleDateFormat.format
      (mEndDateCalendar.getTime()));
    }
    dialog.dismiss();

    if (mStartDateCalendar != null &&
    mEndDateCalendar != null &&
    mClient.isConnected() && !isStartDate) {
      if (mDataPointList.size() > 0) {
          mDataPointList.clear();
      }
      if (mAggregateDataTypeList.size() > 0) {
          mAggregateDataTypeList.clear();
      }
```

```
          isDataAggregated =
          mAggregateCheckBox.isChecked();
          new ReadFromHistoryTask().execute();
        }
      }
});
cancel.setOnClickListener(new View.OnClickListener()
{
  @Override
  public void onClick(View arg0) {
    dialog.dismiss();
  }
});
dialog.show();
}
```

3. The third task performed by `HistoryActivity` is to query the history fitness data and display the results to the user interface. We query the history data inside the `ReadFromHistoryTask` class, which is an instance of `AsyncTask` and is a form of background thread managed by the Android platform. We create two different types of queries, the first with the date interval and the aggregation of data, and the second with only the date interval without aggregation. The first query with the aggregation of data is written inside the `if` block controlled by the `isDataAggregated` Boolean variable and the second query is written in the `else` block. The fitness platform supports two types of `DataType`, normal and aggregate. The normal `DataType` is an individual unit of measurement, while the aggregate `DataType` is an accumulation of units for a particular time interval. Only some of `DataType` support their corresponding aggregate `DataType`, which can be found by using the `DataType.getAggregatesForInput()` method. We input the selected `DataType` in the `getAggregatesForInput()` method; if the input `DataType` supports the aggregate `DataType`, then the list of the corresponding aggregate `DataType` will be returned. If it isn't supported, then an empty list will be returned. One single `DataType` can have multiple corresponding aggregated `DataType`. We only fire the aggregation query if there is a corresponding aggregated `DataType` available for the selected `DataType`, otherwise we show the relevant error message in the `mResultsText` label. The aggregation query consists of two steps. The first step is to create an object of `DataReadRequest` and the second step is to input the `DataReadRequest` object to the `readData()` method of History API. The `DataReadRequest` object is created using the builder syntax, which is shown in the following code snippet. It accepts multiple parameters, such as the start and end time range, the normal `DataType`, and its corresponding aggregated `DataType`. It also accepts the condition by which the aggregation should take place, which is provided by the `bucketByTime()` method. For our example, we will aggregate the data in buckets of one day. The `readData()` method of History API can provide you results in a synchronous call, which is executed using the `await()` method, which itself blocks the thread until the request is completed. Inside the `else` block of the `isDataAggregated` Boolean check, we write the simple query with just the date interval but without the aggregation of data. This query uses the same `DataReadRequest` object, which is passed to the `readData()` method of History API. The major difference between a simple query and an aggregated query is that in a simple query, we only input the date range and selected `DataType` in the object of `DataReadRequest`:

```
public class ReadFromHistoryTask extends
AsyncTask<Void, Void, Void> {
```

```
protected Void doInBackground(Void... params) {

long endTime = mEndDateCalendar.getTimeInMillis();
long startTime =
mStartDateCalendar.getTimeInMillis();
DataReadResult dataReadResult = null;
if(isDataAggregated) {
  mAggregateDataTypeList.addAll(DataType
  .getAggregatesForInput(mSelectedDataType));
  if(mAggregateDataTypeList.size()>0) {
    DataReadRequest readRequest = new
    DataReadRequest.Builder()
    .aggregate(mSelectedDataType,
    mAggregateDataTypeList.get(0))
    .bucketByTime(1, TimeUnit.DAYS)
    .setTimeRange(startTime, endTime,
     TimeUnit.MILLISECONDS).build();
     dataReadResult = Fitness.HistoryApi.readData
     (mClient,readRequest).await();
   } else {
     runOnUiThread(new Runnable() {
       @Override
         public void run() {
           mResultsText.setText("Aggregation of data
           not supported");
           mListAdapter.notifyDataSetChanged();
         }
     });
   }
  } else {
  DataReadRequest readRequest = new
  DataReadRequest.Builder().read(mSelectedDataType)
  .setTimeRange(startTime, endTime,
  TimeUnit.MILLISECONDS).build();
  dataReadResult = Fitness.HistoryApi.readData
  (mClient, readRequest).await();
  }
  if(isDataAggregated) {
    if(mAggregateDataTypeList.size()>0 &&
    dataReadResult!=null) {
       readBucketValues(dataReadResult);
    }
  } else {
  DataSet dataSet =
  dataReadResult.getDataSet(mSelectedDataType);
  readDataSetValues(dataSet, false);
  }
  return null;
```

```
      }
   }
```

4. The fourth task performed by `HistoryActivity`is to read the results from the aggregated query and update the user interface. The results of the aggregated query are assigned to the object of `DataReadResult`, which is passed to the `readBucketValues()` method to extract the values and display them in the user interface. For the aggregated query, we receive the results in the form of buckets, which are processed inside the `readBucketValues()` method. The result of the simple query (without aggregation) with the date range is also assigned to the `DataReadResult` object. For the simple date range query, we receive the results in the form of data sets, which are extracted from the `DataReadResult` object and are passed to the `readDataSetValues()` method for further processing of the data and to display it in the user interface. All the data is extracted and added to `mDataPointList`, which is the `ArrayList` of `DataPoint`. All the extracted data from History API is shown in the `ListView`, which is populated using `mDataPointList`. The implementation of the `ListAdaptor` and user interface (XML layout files) is provided in the code bundle that comes with this chapter and can be downloaded from the support page for the book. The following is a screenshot from a Nexus 5X device, showing the history of all the steps taken in one month aggregated by days:

```
public void readBucketValues(DataReadResult
dataReadResult) {
  bucketSize = 0;
  for (Bucket bucket : dataReadResult.getBuckets()) {

  List<DataSet> dataSets = bucket.getDataSets();

  for (DataSet dataSet : dataSets) {

    if(dataSet.getDataPoints().size()>0)
    {
        bucketSize++;
        readDataSetValues(dataSet, true);
    }
   }
  }
  updateUIThread(true);
}

public void readDataSetValues(DataSet dataSet, boolean
isBucketData) {
```

```
for (DataPoint mDataPoint : dataSet.getDataPoints()) {
  mDataPointList.add(mDataPoint);
}

if(!isBucketData) {
  updateUIThread(isBucketData);
}
}
```

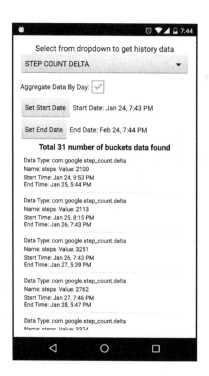

What just happened?

We developed a utility to query history fitness data for a particular selected
`DataType` within a particular date range. The History API is the most important API of all
the Fitness APIs. It works great in combination with Recording API, where the Recording
API instructs the fitness platform to start collecting the data and, through History API, we
retrieve all the collected data. We can aggregate the data using buckets based on four
conditions: time range, session, activity type, and activity segment. Only one condition can
be applied in a bucket at a time for the aggregation of history data.

Asynchronous versus synchronous results callback

Fitness APIs support two modes of operation, asynchronous and synchronous. The asynchronous mode is set by using the `setResultCallback()` method of the APIs that accept the object of `ResultCallback<?>`, inside which the result is delivered whenever it's ready. This asynchronous mode doesn't block the thread. The synchronous mode can be set by using the `await()` method of the APIs. This blocks the thread until the values are returned, so it should never be executed in the main UI thread. Both the `setResultCallback()` and `await()` methods accept a time out as an additional input parameter, which blocks the thread or returns the results object only until the time out period has expired.

Summary

In this chapter, we learned new ways of working with fitness sensors using the Google Fit platform. The Google Fit platform simplifies the whole process of sensor data collection, storage, and retrieval by taking on most of the responsibility itself. The application has to do the minimal work of requesting and querying the fitness data. The Google Fit platform has been developed to deal only with fitness sensor data. It doesn't deal with other sensor data. The Google Fit platform also does a great job of maintaining and syncing all your fitness data on multiple devices, so if you use Android Wear and an Android phone, then both of them track your step counts differently, but at the end of the day you will find that the step count data is the same on both of them.

In the next bonus chapter, we will explore sensors-based APIs and their use in real-world applications. We will also discuss new examples of combining two or more sensors' data together, which is commonly referred to as sensor fusion.

Index